Diagonal (or On-Point) Set

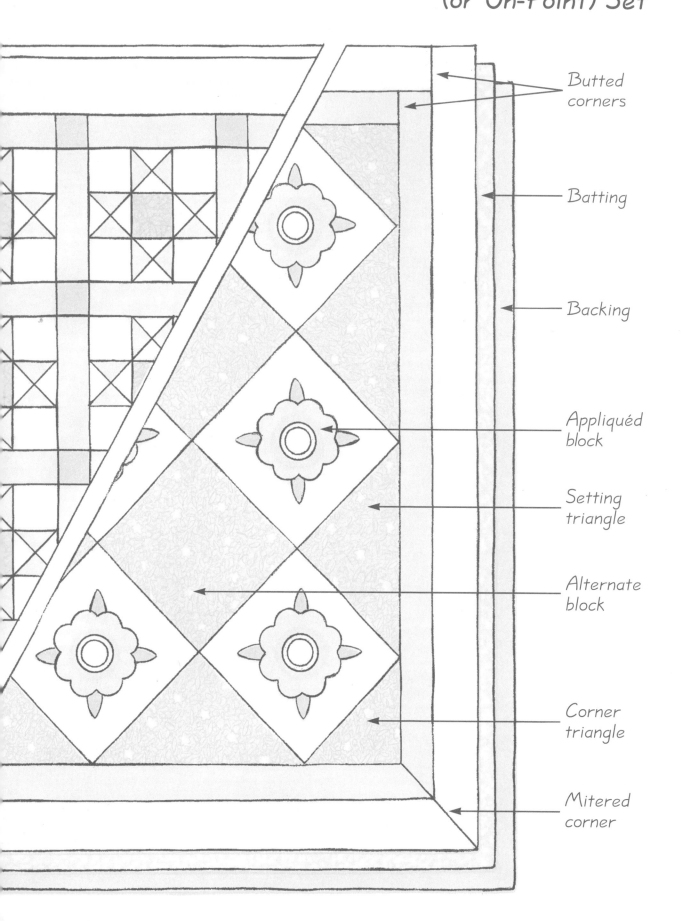

Butted corners

Batting

Backing

Appliquéd block

Setting triangle

Alternate block

Corner triangle

Mitered corner

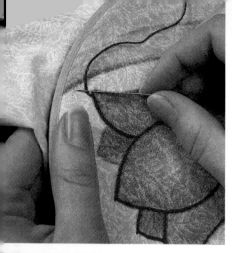

Rodale's Successful
Quilting Library®

Favorite Techniques from the Experts

*Jane Townswick
Editor*

RODALE®

RODALE

WE **INSPIRE** AND **ENABLE** PEOPLE TO IMPROVE
THEIR LIVES AND THE WORLD AROUND THEM

The writers and editors who compiled this book have tried to make all of the contents as accurate and as correct as possible. Illustrations, photographs, and text have all been carefully checked and cross-checked. However, due to the variability of personal skill, tools, materials, and so on, neither the writers nor Rodale Inc. assumes any responsibility for any injuries suffered or for damages or other losses incurred that result from the material presented herein. All instructions should be carefully studied and clearly understood before beginning any project.

Printed in the United States of America on acid-free ∞ , recycled ♻ paper

We're always happy to hear from you.

For questions or comments concerning the editorial content of this book, please write to:

Rodale Book Readers' Service
33 East Minor Street
Emmaus, PA 18098

Look for other Rodale books wherever books are sold. Or call us at (800) 848-4735.

For more information about Rodale and the books and magazines we publish, visit our World Wide Web site at:

www.rodale.com

On the cover: Detail, Still Life #1, by Darra Duffy Williamson
On these pages: Better Cheddar, by Sharyn Craig
On the Contents pages: Spool of Thread, by Laura Heine

Book Producer: Eleanor Levie, Craft Services, LLC
Art Director: Lisa J. F. Palmer
Editor: Jane Townswick
Contributing Editor: Karen Costello Soltys
Writers: Diane Bartels, Cindy A. Blackberg, Georgia J. Bonesteel, Elsie M. Campbell, Karen Kay Buckley, Karen Combs, Sharyn Craig, Jill Sutton Filo, Laura Heine, Jeana Kimball, Suzanne Marshall, Linda Pool, Sally Schneider, Anita Shackelford, Ami Simms, Susan Stein, Mary Stori, Eileen Jahnke Trestain, Beth Wheeler, and Darra Duffy Williamson
Photographer: John P. Hamel
Illustrator: Mario Ferro
Copy Editor: Erana Bumbardatore
Indexer: Nan N. Badgett
Model: Natalie Mering
Hand model: Melanie Sheridan

Rodale Inc.
Editorial Manager, Quilt Continuity: Ellen Pahl
Studio Manager: Leslie M. Keefe
Manufacturing Manager: Mark Krahforst
Manufacturing Coordinator: Patrick T. Smith
Photography Editor: James A. Gallucci
Series Designer: Sue Gettlin

Library of Congress
Cataloging-in-Publication Data

Favorite techniques from the experts / Jane Townswick, editor.
    p. cm. — (Rodale's successful quilting library)
    Includes index.
    ISBN 1–57954–193–3 hardcover
    1. Patchwork. 2. Appliqué. 3 Quilting.
I. Townswick, Jane. II. Series.
TT835.F3867 2000
746.46—dc21   00–035285

Distributed in the book trade by St. Martin's Press

2 4 6 8 10 9 7 5 3 1 hardcover

Contents

Introduction

The first quilt I ever made was a baby quilt, a gift for a friend's first grandchild. When I came up with the idea, I decided that my first project should be a wholecloth quilt. Realizing that if I disliked the actual process of hand quilting, this was likely to be the only quilt I'd ever make, I was determined that it was going to be fun.

Having heard somewhere that newborn babies responded positively to bright colors, I started out by selecting a fire-engine red polyester fabric. To mark an intricate quilting design, I made a trip to a local art supply store for a soft artist's pencil. I didn't notice the smears of graphite covering me from wrists to elbows until after I had finished marking the entire quilt top. I used polyester thread, the thickest batting on the market, and basting needles for quilting.

As you can imagine, my first quilt was a disaster. However, in spite of all the ghastly mistakes I made, the whole process did turn out to be fun, and I presented the finished result proudly to my friend. Watching her little grandson drag that quilt around cheerfully during his first four years of life gave me some of the most enjoyable moments I've ever had.

My quilting did improve over the years, and handwork, both in quilting and appliqué, continued to be my favorite aspect of quiltmaking, as it is to this day. The soothing, almost meditative experience that hand stitching offers has become so much a part of my daily life that I would never want to give it up. I now teach hand appliqué classes that attract students from all over who love the same sorts of techniques that I do.

As I look back, I truly wish I had known any one of the quiltmakers in this book when I made that first wholecloth quilt. My awkward efforts could have been guided and shaped by their expertise. In this book, we share with you some of the favorite quiltmaking techniques of 20 women who are truly masters of their craft. Because of their skills and extensive experience, they have been able to determine the very best methods for accomplishing many different types of quiltmaking tasks. But the methods they present here are their favorites not just because they lead to the kinds of quilts they love, but also because these experts simply enjoy doing them.

As someone who favors handwork, I can certainly appreciate the finely honed lessons of hand piecing points and curves in this book. I see the benefits that await hand appliqué fans in "Template-Free Appliqué," "Take-Away Appliqué," "Cutwork Lace," and "Touches of Elegance: Dimensional Flowers." And whether you quilt by hand or by machine, you'll marvel at the smart freezer paper method of marking quilting designs on borders.

There are also some unusual techniques in this book that may soon become new favorites of mine; I'm eager to try sun printing on a bright summer day. With all of the wonderful shapes Mother Nature has to offer, the idea of using the sun to help create original leaf prints for my quilts is irresistible. I'm counting on the

chapters about crazy patch quilting and embellishments to help me make an elegant Christmas wall quilt for my home next year. And with "Quick-Pieced Kaleidoscopes," "Corner Cutters: A Spinning Success," and "Free-Motion Flourishes" to choose from, I may actually be able to make a quilt for my bedroom—and get it finished before the *next* millennium celebration rolls around.

No matter what your quiltmaking interests are, you're likely to fall in love with the tips, tricks, and methods of the stars in this book, just as I have. Their talents and willingness to share what they know make it easier for all of us quilt-lovers to refine and to increase our skills, and to achieve better results in our quilts. Thank goodness for the touch of these masters' hands—let their expert guidance inspire you, and help you develop your own favorite techniques and explore the possibilities in new ones. Your quiltmaking skills will grow with each new project you make.

Happy quilting!

Jane Townswick

Jane Townswick
Editor

INTRODUCTION

Easy Piecing:
Stars 'n Stripes

Georgia Bonesteel, one of the quilting world's most well-known stars, is famous for her lap quilting technique. Recently she's added another winner to her bag of tricks, some jaunty, free-spirited stars. While these five-pointed stars can be difficult to appliqué or piece, Georgia has developed a technique that simplifies the designing, drafting, and piecing of this star, either within a square or a rectangle. She loves designing with these stars, and her instructions will enable you to star spangle your next quilt or add patriotic pizzazz to a garment.

Getting Ready

To draft your star, draw the block shape onto a gridded freezer paper product called Grid Grip (available in quilt shops, or see "Resources" on page 126). The lines on Grid Grip will ensure perfectly square blocks and help you position pieces on fabric with respect to grain. You can use regular freezer paper instead; you will simply need to mark lines on the paper to help you align templates with the grain of the fabric. Other than Grid Grip or freezer paper, this technique calls only for simple drafting tools that you probably have on hand in your supply of quilting equipment.

The blocks you make can be any size you choose; these instructions feature a 9-inch-square block. Whatever dimension you use should be easily divisible by three. The key to ease in piecing the stars is to code the various sections of the star block carefully and pay attention to grain. The star sections are cut apart, pressed onto fabric, and then cut out, adding the ¼-inch seam allowance on all sides.

What You'll Need

Fabrics for background

Fabrics for star

Grid Grip (or freezer paper)

Pencil

Eraser

Felt-tip marker

Colored pencils

Rotary cutting supplies

Iron

Sewing machine

Thread

Drafting the Stars

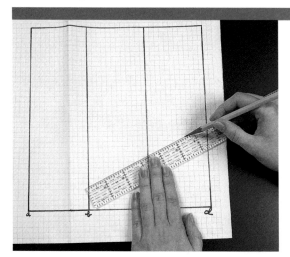

With a felt-tip marker and ruler, draw a 9-inch square on the gridded, nonwaxy side of the Grid Grip (or freezer paper). Follow the marked grid lines on the Grid Grip paper, which will indicate the straight grain of your fabric. Divide the square vertically into three equal rectangles (or rows), drawing these lines with a marker and ruler. Label the vertical lines a, b, c, and d. **Starting on the b line, at or about one inch from the bottom, use a pencil and ruler to draw a diagonal line over to the d line.**

2

Tip

Remember
that your star
will be unique
and have
its own
personality; it's
supposed to
be irregular!

Using the pencil and ruler, continue marking as follows: **Beginning at the d line where your first diagonal line ends, draw a line crossing over both center lines and extending to line a. Next, draw a line from a to d,** passing through the intersection of the first drawn line and line c.

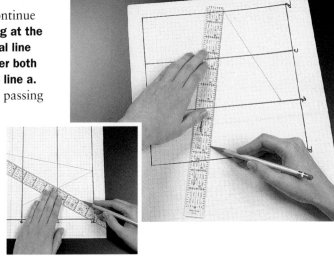

3

Complete the star by drawing from line d to line b, crossing over c where the previous line intersects. **This star is the pattern for making as many star-filled blocks as you desire.** If the last line extends over the outside of the square or one of your star points is cut off, the angle between two lines is too narrow or too wide. Erase the lines and start over. **Shade your star and background with colored pencils to see** what your block will look like in fabric and remind you which fabric to use for each piece.

4

Tip

If you are
using plain
freezer paper,
draw horizontal
or vertical
arrows on
the pieces for
grain
alignment.

To simplify piecing, forget about lines a, b, c, and d, and think of the three vertical rows from left to right as A, B, and C. Some lines within B and C were needed for drafting the star, but aren't needed to piece it. Erase these lines or write "no" over them. To indicate placement and piecing order in the rows, **label the star and background pieces with letters and numbers.** In areas where matching might be tricky, add marks like diamonds or rectangles between pieces to show where templates join. These will come in handy for pinning sections together.

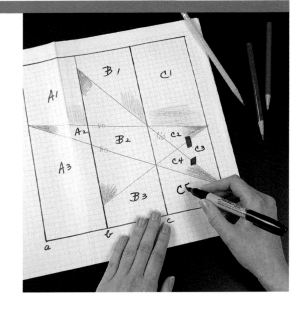

Piecing the Stars

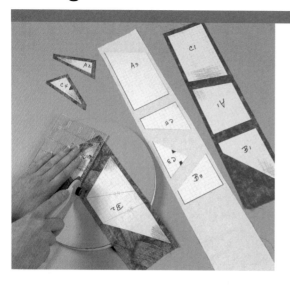

Cut the rows of the star block apart and cut out each template. Cut fabric strips ½ inch wider than the rows for the background and stars—3½ inches in this example. Arrange the templates on the wrong side of your fabrics, referring to the colored templates; align the grid or grain line arrows with the fabric grain. Leave ¼ inch around each template. Press the templates to the fabric. **With a rotary cutter and ruler, cut around the templates, adding an exact ¼-inch seam allowance on each side.**

Tip

Layer other background and star fabrics underneath to cut two or three block's worth of patches at a time.

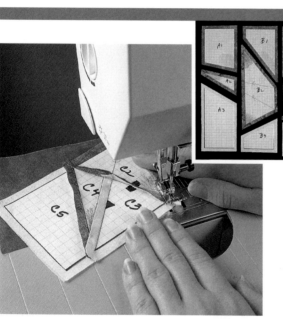

Arrange the A, B, and C rows in their numbered sequences next to your sewing machine. Place the right sides of two adjacent patches from row A together. Pin the patches together, matching the grid lines and aligning the marks. Leave the paper templates in place, and stitch along the edges. Stitch the numbered segments of row A together. Do not stitch through the paper on the underneath side. **Stitch the patches in rows B and C together in the same manner.** Finally, pin and sew all the rows together. Peel off the templates and reuse them.

Tip

Iron the same templates to any underlying patches you cut before, and repeat the piecing process to make more blocks.

Press the completed block carefully, and you're on your way to stardom! You can also use the same basic technique to piece a star in a rectangle, by simply extending the rows of the square. For the Stars and Strips bomber jacket on page 8, Georgia Bonesteel added strips to rectangular star blocks until a section was large enough for each pattern piece of the garment.

Tip

Make several rectangular star blocks, and arrange the rectangles in rows to make a quilt top.

EASY PIECING: STARS 'N STRIPES

11

Quick-Pieced
Kaleidoscopes

Do you remember when you first discovered the enchantment inside a kaleidoscope? Shifting patterns and constantly changing colors make these classic childhood toys a never-ending source of delight, and they have long been a source of inspiration for creative quilt designs for Sally Schneider. You'll love her method of using grids to quick-piece the versatile Kaleidoscope pattern. And you'll recapture the childlike sense of fun that comes from playing with blocks—quilt blocks, that is!

Getting Ready

Taking a hands-on approach and going through the piecing process will make learning this great grid technique fast, fun, and easy. Follow the steps in this chapter for piecing the Kaleidoscope block in an 8-inch-square format. You can choose any color scheme; you'll simply need a dark and a light fabric for the wedge shapes, and the same light fabric for the corner triangles. With the fabrics listed in "What You'll Need," you'll be able to make up to six Kaleidoscope blocks.

You'll need a special ruler for marking angled lines over a simple grid. Use the 8-inch Kaleido-Ruler for Kaleidoscope blocks up to 8 inches square, or purchase a similar item from your local quilt shop.

What You'll Need

18 × 22-inch piece of dark fabric, for wedges

18 × 22-inch piece of light fabric, for wedges

3¼ × 22-inch strip of same light fabric, for corner triangles

Iron and ironing board

Fabric-marking pen or pencil

8-inch Kaleido-Ruler

Sewing machine

¼" presser foot (optional)

Neutral color thread for piecing

Rotary cutter and mat

6 × 24-inch acrylic ruler

Silk pins

Step-by-Step Kaleidoscopes

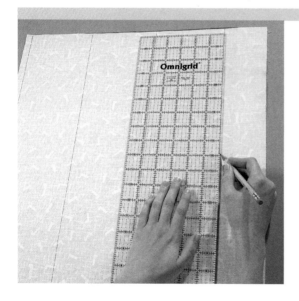

1

To begin making an 8-inch Kaleidoscope block, place the two 18 × 22-inch fabrics for the wedges together with right sides facing. Lay them on a pressing surface with the lighter fabric on top, and press them lightly with a hot, dry iron to make them "stick" together. Move them to a flat surface, and mark a line ½ inch in from one long edge of the fabric. **Mark three more lines parallel to the first, spacing the lines exactly 4⅞ inches apart.** Rotate the fabric carefully so that the lines are horizontal and the first line you drew is at the top.

2

Align the 8-inch line on the Kaleido-Ruler with the second marked horizontal line, at the left side of the fabric. The top edge of the ruler will not touch the first marked line. **Mark a line on both sides of the ruler that extends toward your first marked line, keeping the pencil almost parallel to the fabric.** (This helps the pencil roll more smoothly, without wrinkling or distorting the fabric, and it keeps the point sharper.) **Move the ruler up and use it to extend these two lines to meet exactly at your first marked line.**

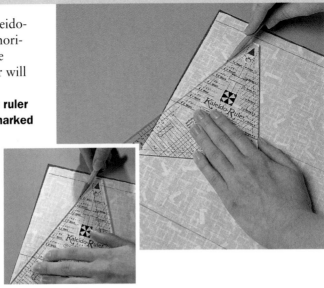

3

Place a 6 x 24-inch acrylic ruler over the marked triangle, so that the ruler's right edge touches the lower right corner of the triangle you just drew. The vertical lines on the ruler should be parallel to the left side of the triangle. **Mark a line from the first horizontal line you drew all the way to the fourth. Measure the distance from this line to the left side of the triangle, and continue marking parallel lines across the fabric, spacing them this far apart.** For an 8-inch block, this distance will be exactly 3¾ inches.

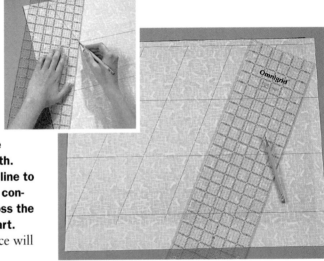

4

Draw a second set of parallel lines all the way across the fabric, this time in the opposite direction. To do this, align the right edge of the ruler with the right side of the marked triangle; it should also pass through all of the intersections of horizontal lines and angled lines. **The marking of the grid is now complete.**

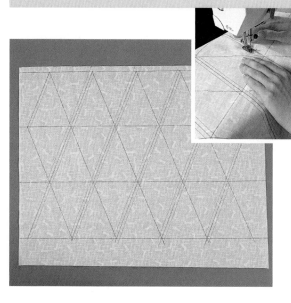

If your fabrics have shifted or become distorted during the marking process, realign and press them again. **On only the left sides of the marked triangles, stitch a ¼-inch seam on both sides of the angled lines.** (Sewing on the *left* sides of the triangles and pressing these seam allowances toward the dark fabric after they are cut apart will make the seam allowances face the proper direction to nest together accurately in the finished Kaleidoscope block.) Note that the outside triangles don't require a double line of stitching.

After stitching the angled seams, press the fabrics again, and place them on a cutting mat. **Using a 6 × 24-inch acrylic ruler, rotary-cut along the marked grid lines**. Take care to cut accurately, so that the resulting pairs of wedges will all be the correct size. If there are a few stitches remaining on the corner of a wedge pair, pull the wedges apart very gently to remove the threads. **After cutting the pairs of wedges apart, open them up and press the seam allowances toward the darker fabric.**

Trim the points from the seam allowance for easier matching. Place two pairs of wedges right sides together, with the seam allowances between the top pair of wedges pressed to the left, and the seam allowances of the bottom pair pressed to the right. The presser foot will push the top seam allowance against the ridge of the one underneath and they'll stay correctly positioned. **Then stitch the pairs of wedges together.** Sew slowly to avoid stretching the bias edges. This completes half of a Kaleidoscope block. Repeat for the other half.

Tip

If you don't have a ¼-inch presser foot, mark the seam allowances to make sure they are accurate.

Tip

When you make lots of Kaleidoscope blocks for a quilt, chain-stitch the wedge pairs together, without cutting the thread at the end of each seam.

QUICK-PIECED KALEIDOSCOPES

Place two half-block units right sides together. **Place a pin through the top layer at the center seam intersection.** Insert the pin through the bottom center seam intersection and pull the pin tight to align the centers. Don't bring the point of the pin back up through the fabric, as this could shift the alignment. Place a second and third pin through the fabric on either side of the first pin. Stitch the seam, removing the pins just before the needle reaches them, so that the needle goes exactly through the intersection of the seams. **Press these seam allowances open.**

For the corner triangles, start by cutting two 3¼-squares of the same light fabric as you used for the Kaleidoscope triangles **and then cut each square in half diagonally.** If you are making several blocks, cut multiple squares and half square triangles from a 3¼ × 22-inch strip.

Center the corner triangles on each corner of the block and pin them to the wedges. Since the long edges of the corner triangles are on the bias, **sew with the corner triangles on the bottom,** so that the presser foot won't stretch these edges. **Using a ¼-inch seam allowance, stitch across each corner to complete the Kaleidoscope block.**

The Quilter's
Problem Solver

Just My Size

Problem	Solution
You want to make Kaleidoscope blocks in several sizes, but don't know how to calculate the right size for marking the grid lines or cutting the corner triangles.	Start by deciding what size blocks you want to make. To determine the size of the grid you'll need, divide that measurement in half, and then add $\frac{7}{8}$ inch for seam allowances. For corner triangles, there's no standard formula; use the sizes provided in the following chart, or simply cut your corner triangles larger than necessary, and trim them even with the edges of your finished blocks after sewing them on.

Finished Block Size	Distance between First Grid Lines	Squares for Corner Triangles
8" square	4⅞"	3¼"
7" square	4⅜"	2⅞"
6" square	3⅞"	2⅝"
5" square	3⅜"	2⅜"
4" square	2⅞"	2⅛"

Problem	Solution
After sewing the two halves of a Kaleidoscope block together, the seam does not lie flat.	Remove the stitching between the halves of the Kaleidoscope block with a seam ripper. Check the long, straight edge on the two pairs of triangles. If it's not straight, place an acrylic ruler over one half-block, and mark a *straight* seam line that intersects with the center point. Pin this half-block to the other half-block with right sides together, matching centers, and stitch exactly on your marked line, to make the finished block straight and true.

Skill Builder

Challenge yourself to use your Kaleidoscope blocks in different ways.

Make up several blocks in various color combinations of your choice. Arrange them on a design wall in different configurations. Each time, step back and consider how the blocks look together, and take Polaroids so you can keep track of your experiments. You can also photocopy and enlarge the black-and-white illustration (below, far right), and use colored pencils to try out various color combinations, using two colors—or more.

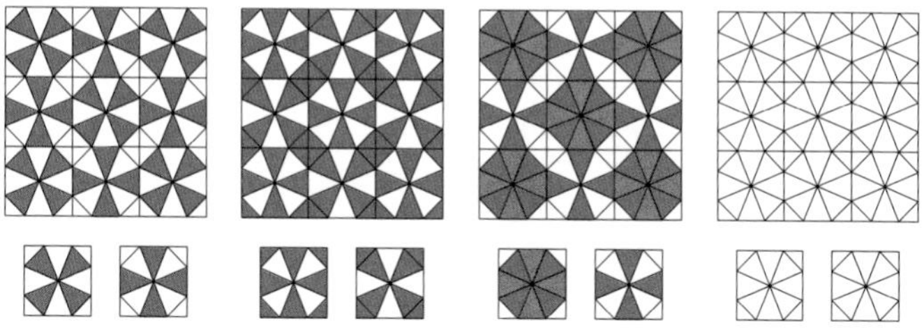

Try This!

Kick the Kaleidoscope block up a notch with fabric variations.

Vary the fabrics you layer for the wedge shapes. Choose high-contrast darks and lights, or darks and brights. Cut from smaller pieces of fabric; calculate the grid size needed for your block size. Count the wedges you'll need for each block, and cut fabrics large enough for as many wedges as you'll need. Cut corner triangles from different fabrics, so you can include more colors. Don't repeat fabrics, and mix up pairs of wedges when you make the blocks.

QUICK-PIECED KALEIDOSCOPES

Log Cabin—
with Attitude!

Be forewarned: Darra Duffy Williamson's favorite freewheeling flowers may put a
serious dent in your scrap bag. And Darra cautions that piecing them is like eating
peanuts—once you start, it's hard to stop! Appliquéing these fanciful Log Cabin
blossoms onto a background fabric is easy with fusible web, and it takes only a fraction of
the time required for more traditional appliqué methods. You may find yourself dreaming
of these fun flowers in vases and baskets, and tumbling out of the corners of your next quilt.

Getting Ready

To learn this technique, follow the step-by-step instructions to make a sample block. Select fabric for a background square and an assortment of colorful fabrics for the Log Cabin flowers. You'll also need a lightweight, iron-on fusible web. Ask a salesperson at your local quilt shop for advice, and consider experimenting with different brands before you make your choice. Whichever brand of fusible web you select, be sure to test various factors including proper iron temperature; how long to apply heat; and if, when, and how to use a press cloth or nonstick pressing sheet. All can affect the ability of any fusible web to adhere two layers of fabric together easily.

For color inspiration for your Log Cabin flowers, visit botanical gardens, nurseries, or garden centers. Collect photographs, greeting cards, and postcards, and study photos and illustrations in gardening magazines and flower and bulb catalogs.

What You'll Need

- **Square of fabric for background**
- **Assorted colorful scrap fabrics**
- **Rotary cutting equipment**
- **Fabric scissors**
- **Sewing machine**
- **Basic sewing supplies**
- **Neutral-color thread**
- **Thread snips or embroidery scissors**
- **Iron and ironing board**
- **Spray starch or spray sizing**
- **Lightweight iron-on fusible web**
- **Nonstick pressing sheet**
- **Decorative threads for embellishments (optional)**

Log Cabin Flowers

1

Use your fabric scissors or rotary cutter to cut out a center for your first Log Cabin flower. **Cut an irregularly shaped, four-sided patch with straight edges.** It should not be a perfect square or rectangle. This irregularity adds interest, and is more in keeping with the whimsical nature of these flowers.

Tip

Look at a the way colors are combined in a selection of seed packets to plan a color palette for your Log Cabin flowers.

2

Select a piece of fabric for your first flower "petal." Since this is a "sew-first, then cut" technique, you can use any odd-shaped piece of fabric, first straightening one edge, if necessary. Align the raw edge of your petal fabric with one side of your cut center piece, with right sides together. The petal fabric should be longer than the flower center and extend a bit beyond both sides of the center piece. **Sew the two fabrics together with a ¼-inch seam allowance,** and press the seam allowance away from the center.

3

Place the pressed unit on a cutting mat and align an acrylic ruler with an adjacent, unstitched side of the center piece. Use a rotary cutter to trim the excess petal fabric. **Trim the excess petal fabric on the other side in the same way, by aligning the ruler with the opposite side of the center piece.** It is essential that these first two cuts follow the angle of the center piece. This will allow you to maintain a four-sided shape throughout the construction of your flower.

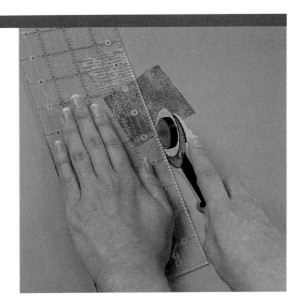

4

Use a rotary cutter and ruler to trim the *outside* edge of your first petal at any odd angle you like. It isn't necessary to make this cut match the angled edge of the center piece; in fact, your flower will be more free-form and natural if it does not. This edge will be the outer edge of the completed flower. As you trim, keep the size of the center piece and the desired finished size of the flower in mind, so your finished flower will be nicely proportioned.

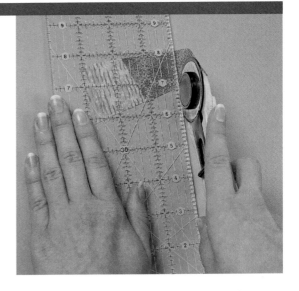

Proceeding clockwise around the center piece, continue adding petals to the remaining three sides, in typical Log Cabin fashion. Before you stitch, make sure that the ends of each petal you add extend beyond the center unit. **Trim each petal after stitching, maintaining the angles established by the raw edges of the previous piece.** Press all seam allowances away from the center, so that the block will lie flat.

No seam rippers required! Use your rotary cutter to trim away an unwanted petal and be content with a smaller flower center.

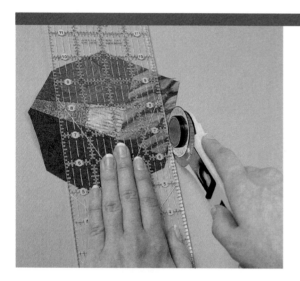

Shape your stitched Log Cabin flower by angling an acrylic ruler over each corner of your block. **Using your rotary cutter, trim the corners randomly, trying out a variety of tilts and angles before you actually cut.** Cut each corner at a slightly different angle, so your finished flower has a natural look.

Since most outside edges of the block are cut on the bias, avoid stretching your Log Cabin flower. **For added stability, apply a light coating of spray starch or spray sizing just before you press.** Handle the block as gently as possible, and press it by lifting and repositioning (rather than

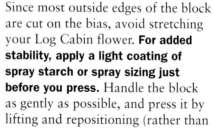

dragging) an iron across the surface. If, despite your best efforts, the flower becomes misshapen before you are ready to fuse it to the background, **use your rotary cutter and ruler to trim it back into shape.**

LOG CABIN—WITH ATTITUDE!

8

Cut a piece of fusible web slightly larger than your Log Cabin flower. Position the fusible web rough side up (paper side down), on a pressing surface. Center your flower right side up on top. Place a nonstick pressing sheet over both; this will protect your iron. **Press to fuse the web in place,** following the manufacturer's instructions for the fusible web. **Trim the fusible web even with the raw edges of your Log Cabin flower,** and remove the paper backing.

9

Press fusible web onto pieces of fabric to make leaves and a stem. **Use a pair of scissors to cut free-form stems and leaves for your Log Cabin flower.** Free yourself from the notion of needing a pattern— the more imaginatively you shape your leaves and stem, the more charming your Log Cabin flower block will be. Experiment with your Log Cabin flowers, stems, and leaves to determine where to position these shapes on your background. When you are happy with the arrangement of your design, **use an iron to fuse the shapes in place.**

10

For a little extra "attitude," add some decorative hand and machine stitching to your design. Use heavy threads to embroider tendrils and stars in the flower centers. Use rayon or metallic threads to straight-stitch close to the appliquéd edges, which will keep the fused shapes from lifting from the surface. You may prefer to do this after you layer your quilt top, so you can simultaneously quilt around each shape.

The Quilter's
Problem Solver

A Sticky Situation

Problem	Solution
Oops! You've fused too enthusiastically, and now you have fusible "gunk" all over your iron.	Don't fret—everyone who uses fusible web presses the wrong side or forgets to use a pressing sheet at one time or another! A product like Dritz Iron-Off or Fabricraft Hot Iron Cleaner will remove sticky buildup from your iron. You can also use materials already on hand—such as a used fabric softener sheet. Set your iron to a medium-high setting, and press the iron plate over the sheet until all of the fusible sticky stuff is gone.

Skill Builder

Make off-kilter Log Cabin with Attitude blocks that are square, to resemble more traditional scrappy Log Cabins blocks.

Gather several fabrics in a wide variety of colors and prints. Construct the block as described in Steps 2 through 6, but don't trim the corners. Add extra rounds to the block, and cut the final round *extra wide*. Use a square acrylic ruler to trim the block to the size you want. Arrange your squared-up blocks in any number of exciting sets.

Try This!

Let your imagination soar with Log Cabin blossoms!

Besides the obvious quilts, wallhangings, and pillows, use Log Cabin with Attitude flowers to embellish vests, jackets, skirt hems, evening bags, and totes. Frame them with appliquéd (or fused) leaves and vines, or "plant" them in fabric vases and pots. Embellish their centers with colorful buttons. Use clear crystal beads for glistening dew drops. Bugle beads make wonderful thorns, while fancy threads and stitchery suggest tendrils and ferns. Try some couching, silk ribbon embroidery, paint, stencils, rubber stamps, charms...the possibilities are endless.

LOG CABIN—WITH ATTITUDE!

Crazy Quilting
by Machine

In Karen Kay Buckley's wall hanging, her "Opulent Ornaments" glow with luminous satins and silks. In this chapter, Karen shows you her favorite way to do crazy quilting. It's easy to stitch crazy-quilt patchwork ornaments by machine, embellishing them with laces, ribbons, cording, and trims. The background of her wall quilt is reverse appliqué; the green print is so rich, you can almost catch the scent of pine needles in the room. Since you'll do everything by machine, in very little time you can have an elegant holiday quilt to enjoy for years to come.

Getting Ready

Consider the many and varied fabrics you can use for crazy-quilt patchwork ornaments. In addition to lush velvets, soft silks, and shiny satins, think about including decorator prints, polyesters, rayons, lamé, and anything else unusual that strikes your fancy. Look for fabrics with interesting tactile qualities and visual textures. Karen's ivory palette is sleek and sophisticated; however, you may prefer to think about the effects you could create with rich jewel tones.

If your sewing machine can do a wide array of decorative stitches, this is the perfect chance to put it through its paces! For reverse appliqué by machine, a blind stitch is helpful, but not required—you can achieve good results with narrow zigzag stitches. For decorative stitching with metallic threads, use 60/8 Microtex needles. Their larger eye and sharper point will make for a smoother, easier job, with fewer thread breaks.

What You'll Need

- **Silks, satins, and velvets**
- **8-inch-square muslin base**
- **8-inch background square**
- **2 × 3-inch gold lamé**
- **4-inch length of ⅛-inch-wide gold ribbon**
- **Laces, ribbons, and cording**
- **Fine, permanent marker**
- **Template plastic**
- **Paper scissors**
- **Pencil and acrylic ruler**
- **60/8 Microtex needles**
- **Neutral thread for crazy piecing**
- **Thread to match background fabric**
- **Decorative threads**
- **YLI .004 clear nylon thread**
- **Water-soluble glue stick**
- **Sewing machine**

Crazy Piecing

1

Using a fine, permanent marker, trace the ornament pattern on page 29 (including the small, green lines at the top and bottom) onto a piece of template plastic, and cut it out. To prepare the fabric foundation, use a pencil and draw a diagonal line from corner to corner on the square of muslin. Make a small mark 1½ inches up from one end of this line. **Trace the ornament shape onto the muslin square so that the center of the bottom of the ornament lies on this mark, and the top is also centered on the diagonal line.**

2

Select a fabric you want to place at the center of your crazy patch ornament. Using fabric scissors, cut out a shape roughly 2½ inches square or a rectangle approximately 1½ × 2½ inches from this fabric; cut the edges straight. Next, cut off one corner of this shape, creating a five-sided shape with uneven sides. **Pin this shape at the center of the ornament outline marked on the muslin base.**

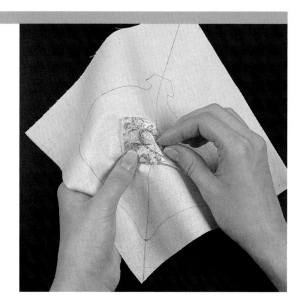

3

Tip

Finger press crazy-patch seams, rather than pressing them with a hot iron, because many decorative fabrics are heat-sensitive.

From a different fabric, cut a second piece that is longer than any side of the first piece. Place it on the first piece, with right sides together, even with any edge *except* the fifth side (the odd angle you cut last). Sew these pieces together using a ¼-inch seam allowance. Unfold the second piece and finger-crease the seam. Prepare for the next crazy patch: Use a pencil and an acrylic ruler to mark a line extending from the edge of piece number 1 across piece number 2, and **trim away the excess fabric beyond this line, using a pair of scissors.**

4

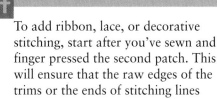

Tip

Test-sew decorative stitches on scraps of the same fabric you're using.

To add ribbon, lace, or decorative stitching, start after you've sewn and finger pressed the second patch. This will ensure that the raw edges of the trims or the ends of stitching lines will be covered by successive patches. If you add lace, topstitch it in place with clear nylon thread. **For ribbon, match the thread on your machine to the ribbon, and sew a line of fine, straight stitches down each edge.** If you're adding cording, you may need to put a cording foot on your machine. If you decide to omit laces and trims, **consider adding decorative stitches in gold or other metallic threads.**

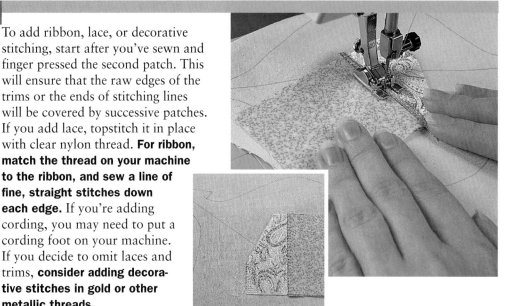

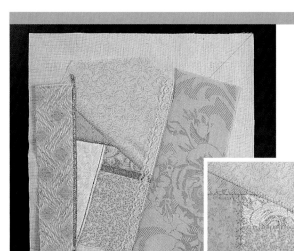

Continue attaching crazy-patch pieces in a circular fashion around the center piece, **adding either more trims, decorative stitching in metallic threads, or both as you go.** Work until the crazy-patch pieces cover the entire ornament shape and extend at least ½ inch beyond the marked edges of the shape, so there will be no gaps when you stitch the background fabric on top.

Fold back the patch at the top of the ornament and use a pencil and ruler to mark a straight horizontal line over the crazy patches at the bottom of the "cap." Position a 2 × 3-inch piece of gold lamé right side down on top of the crazy-patch ornament, with the raw edge extending ¼ inch over the marked line (toward the top of the ornament). Sew the gold lamé to the ornament with a ¼-inch seam allowance. **Fold the gold lamé to its right side, and finger-press the seam.**

Tip

Don't use a hot iron on lamé—this is a synthetic fabric that will melt easily.

Adding a Background Overlay

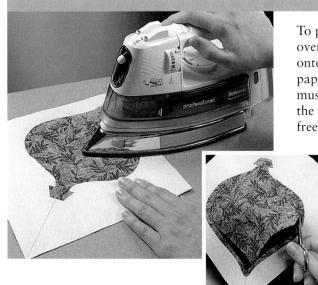

To prepare the background fabric overlay, trace the ornament shape onto an 8-inch square of freezer paper the same way you did for the muslin foundation fabric. Cut out the ornament shape, creating a freezer paper window template with an ornament-shaped opening. **Press this template onto the wrong side of the background fabric square. Cut ⅜ inch to the inside of the ornament shape, leaving seam allowances all around.**

Tip

Wait for the glue to dry before you stitch the background fabric over the crazy patch shape, to avoid getting adhesive in your machine.

2

Clip into the seam allowances at the corners of the ornament cap and along the curves. Make clips at close intervals along the tightest curves of the ornament shape. To prepare the background overlay for machine appliqué, **turn the seam allowances to the wrong side, and use glue stick to adhere the seam allowances to the freezer paper.**

3

For the hanging ribbon at the top of the ornament, lay a 4-inch length of ⅛-inch-wide gold ribbon on the background piece between the center of the ornament cap and the corner of the fabric, tucking ¼ inch to the underside of the cutout for the ornament cap. **Topstitch the ribbon in place along both edges with gold metallic or clear nylon thread. Begin both lines of stitching at the ornament cap and sew outward to the corner.**

4

Center and pin the background fabric overlay on top of the muslin foundation with the crazy-patch ornament. **Reverse appliqué the turned-back edges by machine, using a blind stitch or small zigzag stitch.** Use clear nylon thread in the top of the machine and regular sewing thread to match the background fabric in the bobbin. When the reverse appliqué is complete, trim away the excess muslin base and crazy patch fabric from behind your work, and remove the freezer paper.

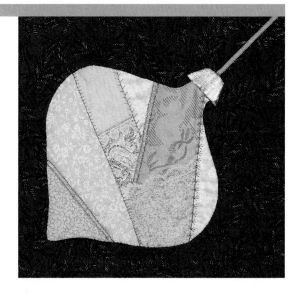

Best Foot Forward

Problem	Solutions
I'm having a problem with buckling, wrinkling, and tangles when topstitching or couching a trim, and don't know what's gone wrong.	The solution might be as simple as using a different presser foot, which can make a huge difference. Try one of these the next time you're having topstitching troubles: ❏ An edge-stitching foot makes sewing along the edge of laces and ribbons easy. ❏ An open-toed embroidery foot is good for decorative stitches, satin stitching, and thin cording. ❏ A bulky overlock foot handles thicker yarns, wools, and pipings nicely. ❏ A braiding foot can be used for raised or padded satin stitching and couching thicker yarns. ❏ A cording foot also works well with thicker yarns. Your needle choice is also important. Use an 80/12 needle, but if that causes puckering, switch to a smaller size 60/8 needle, especially for working with more delicate laces, ribbons, and trims.

Pattern for Ornament
(Actual Size)

CRAZY QUILTING BY MACHINE

Patchwork
Illusions

V isual depth and perspective have fascinated artists for centuries. Intrigued by optical illusions like those found in the works of M.C. Escher, quilt artist Karen Combs has developed a quick and easy rotary cutting technique that allows her to make pieced quilts with a three-dimensional look. Karen shares her secrets, so your quilts, too, can become masterpieces of three-dimensional illusion.

Getting Ready

Simple blocks are the most effective in three-dimensional quilt designs. The block featured in this chapter is a Sawtooth Star, but you can also work with any traditional patchwork pattern you like that is simply pieced with squares or half-square triangles. You'll need a pad of isometric graph paper, so that you can draw your quilt blocks in a nonsquare format. Architectural and drafting supply stores and quilt shops sell this type of graph paper. In addition, you'll need to make or purchase a template for cutting 3-inch, 60-degree diamond shapes. This isometric diamond template, and the isometric graph paper shown in this chapter are available from Karen Combs's Studio. See "Resources" on page 126 for ordering information.

The Values of Dimension

Choosing Fabrics

Selecting fabrics is an essential part of creating pieced designs that have a three-dimensional look. Only when you choose color values (lightness or darkness) correctly can your quilts generate a sense of visual depth. **Look for a light, a medium, and a dark fabric in each of two different color families.** Include some fabrics that are quiet prints, so you can pair them with busier prints.

PATCHWORK ILLUSIONS

31

Drafting a Sawtooth Star

1

Working on regular graph paper and using a pencil and ruler, draw a grid four squares by four squares. Working with the grid lines, connect intersections to draw a Sawtooth Star block. Add a square on point in the middle, as shown on the sketch in blue. Do the same thing again, this time adapting your sketch to the lines on a sheet of isometric graph paper. **After you have drawn one isometric Sawtooth Star block, draw two more adjacent to it, creating a cubelike configuration.**

2

Using colored pencils, shade each of the Sawtooth Star blocks. Choose different colored pencils that correspond to your fabrics, or exert different amounts of pressure to simulate the light, medium, and dark fabrics you've selected. Use the two lightest shades on one block, the two medium shades on another, and the two darkest shades on the third. When combined, the result will *seem* to be a three-dimensional cube of identical sides, with a single source of light hitting the cube from one side and leaving the other sides in shadow.

3

Analyze the design and make a list of the type and number of patches and units you will need to cut for each of the Sawtooth Star blocks in your isometric drawing. An exploded drawing may be helpful. Notice that in some of the diamond units, a seam allowance splits the shape lengthwise, and in other diamond units, there will be a crosswise seam. **Using colored pencils, draw the diamond units needed for each individual Sawtooth Star block, and count the number of each unit you will need.** This will be a handy visual guide for cutting patches and assembling units.

Cutting & Piecing

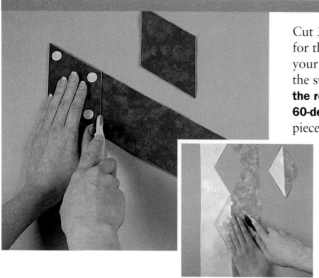

Cut 3-inch strips of each of the fabrics for the unpieced diamond shapes in your Sawtooth Star blocks, and layer the strips on a cutting mat. **Rotary cut the required diamonds, using a 3-inch, 60-degree diamond template.** For the pieced diamond units, cut a 3½ × 44-inch strip from each of the two light, medium, and dark fabrics. Sew the two light strips together, the two mediums together, and the two darks together. Press the seam allowances open. Referring to your drawing, **cut the number of units you need.**

Before rotary cutting, apply spray sizing to the fabric to keep the bias from stretching as you strip piece, cut patches, and sew patches together.

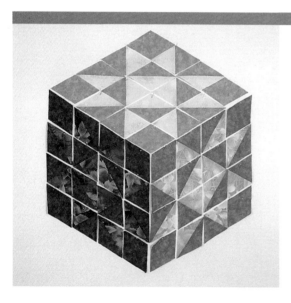

2

After you have cut out all of the patches for your blocks, arrange them on a design wall, referring to your graph paper sketch. View the arrangement from a distance to make sure that all of the lights, mediums, and darks produce the sense of depth shown in your sketch.

After you're sure that all of the patches are positioned where they belong, sew the patches together to produce four rows for each block. **As you pin and sew two patches together, offset them by exactly ¼ inch.** The tips of the acute angle should protrude. Do *not* trim these little tips at either end of the seam. **Press the seam allowances to one side.**

PATCHWORK ILLUSIONS

4

Join the rows of each block, **matching and pinning the seams between patches** and offsetting the end patches by ¼ inch, as before. Press the seam allowances to one side, pressing first from the wrong side, **then from the right side.** Complete each block that will make up the cube.

Tip

Mark the key center point on each seam in your blocks by using a pencil and a ruler before pinning or sewing seams.

5

Think of each side of your cube design as a single, diamond-shaped block. Place two blocks with right sides together, and insert a straight pin exactly ¼ inch from the center point, where all three blocks will come together in the finished cube. Place pins at the seam intersections between patches. **Starting at the center pin, stitch the two blocks together.** Next, set in the third block, sewing from the center out on both sides. **All three seams will start at the center of the cube.**

Center point

6

You can create either a pieced or an appliquéd quilt top from your pieced cube. **The pieced version shown here has dark background fabrics:** Extend the sides of your cube to square off the design. For this cube, cut two 6 × 13-inch rectangles in half to make four half-rectangles. Sew one onto each corner of the cube. Add 1½-inch-wide strips of fabric to the sides, so the cube "floats" in the center. **For appliqué, cut a large background square, and stitch the outer edges of the cube on top.** For either quilt type, add borders all around.

Three-Dimensional Woes

Problem	Solution
You matched the ¼-inch "tails" when sewing together two diamonds, but the seam is rippled or wavy.	The bias edge on the diamond can sometimes stretch out of shape if your template slips slightly. To fix this, use a seam ripper to remove the line of stitching. Place the template on your fabric patch, and trim away any excess fabric from the bias edge of the cut diamond. You may also be able to solve the problem by pinning the rippled side to hold it in the correct position, and sewing with the stretched side against the feed dogs to help ease in the excess.
Your patchwork does not have visual depth to give it the three-dimensional appearance you're looking for.	You need more contrast within and between the three blocks that make up the cube. Vary the fabric prints as well as the color values. Try using distinct, large-scale patterns for the fabrics in one block; hazy, medium-scale patterns for a second block; and mottled or small tone-on-tone prints for the third block.

Skill Builder

Make your own double-duty value finder.

Selecting light, medium, and dark fabrics is much easier if you use the right kind of value finder. Buy a green and a red see-through plastic report cover from an office supply store, and cut a 3 × 5-inch rectangle from each one. Use the red one to test values on all fabrics except red. Use the green value finder on all fabrics except green. For multicolor fabrics, test value by overlapping the green and the red value finders—and looking through both of them!

Try This!

For accuracy—tape your thumb!

When measuring ¼-inch "tails" on small patches, using a ruler can be cumbersome. Try this trick: Place a piece of ¼-inch masking tape on your thumbnail, and lay your taped thumb on the fabric to quickly and accurately measure the ¼-inch distance.

Corner Cutters:
A Spinning Success

Quilt blocks that are not all quite the same size present a challenge when they are to be set together. Sharyn Craig, author and well-known quilting teacher, is always up for any kind of challenge. When a friend presented her with a set of pieced blocks from a quilt guild raffle, Sharyn rose to the task. Here is her fabulous technique for joining inconsistent blocks; her Corner Cutters add a jazzy but unifying setting element as a bonus. Sharyn likes to use this technique for uniform blocks, as well. Read on to discover how cutting corners can be a good thing!

Getting Ready

Blocks from a guild exchange, a workshop, or a block-of-the-month series are all good candidates for learning the Corner Cutters technique. Larger blocks, 8 to 15 inches square, framed with 2- to 3-inch-wide strips will work best with the 3-inch Pinwheel Corner Cutters in this chapter. Try working with these sizes, and then experiment with different sizes of Corner Cutters for larger or smaller blocks. You'll soon be ready to explore other creative variations on your own.

The fabric for framing your blocks does not need to be any of the fabrics in your blocks; any compatible fabric will become a unifying design element. To prepare framing strips for your blocks and borders, cut 3½-inch strips across the full 44-inch width of fabric. As you work, cut these strips to the lengths needed. These strips will help compensate for any slight differences in block sizes.

What You'll Need

At least four quilt blocks (the same or close to the same size)

Fabric for framing strips

Fabric for border strips

Light, medium, and dark fabrics for Corner Cutters (Pinwheel blocks)

Graph paper, 8 squares per inch

Rotary cutter and mat

6-inch square and 6 × 24-inch acrylic rulers

Paper scissors

Scotch brand removable tape

Sewing machine

Basic sewing supplies

Corner Cutters

Sew two 3½-inch-wide framing strips to opposite sides of a block, and trim the strips even with the edges of the block. Press the seam allowances toward the framing strips. **Repeat for the remaining two sides of this block,** trimming these strips even with the edges of the framed block. Again press the seam allowances toward the framing strips. Repeat this process for as many blocks as you want to use in your quilt.

Tip

Be conscious of the fabric's pattern when attaching the framing strips to each block, especially if you're using stripes or plaids.

CORNER CUTTERS: A SPINNING SUCCESS

Tip

Use a single fabric, two different fabrics, or frame each of your blocks differently—anything that pleases you will work.

2

After you add framing strips to each of your blocks, use an acrylic ruler to trim and make sure all the blocks are the same size and perfectly square. Even if you think that your original blocks are identical, there can sometimes be very slight differences that can affect how the blocks will go together. When you start out with blocks that are square and consistent in size, your finished quilt will lie flat.

3

Make a Corner Cutter guide, so that you can trim away a portion of each framing strip consistently and then replace it with a pieced Pinwheel unit. **On a piece of graph paper that has 8 squares per inch, draw a right triangle with the two short sides 3⅛ inches long.** Label this triangle with the finished size of 3 inches. This is a Corner Cutter guide.

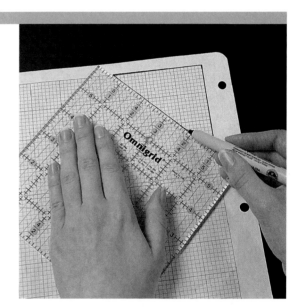

4

Cut out the Corner Cutter guide. **Tape it underneath a 6-inch square acrylic ruler so that the long side of the paper triangle aligns with the edge of the ruler.** (It is not necessary for it to be at a corner.)

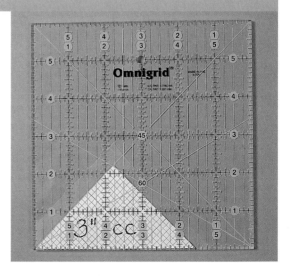

5

Position the 6-inch square ruler so that the two short sides of your Corner Cutter Guide are in alignment with a corner of your framed block. **Trim away the corner of the block.** Repeat this process on all four corners on each of your blocks.

6

Next, assemble the Corner Cutter units that will become Pinwheels when your blocks are stitched together. **Start by cutting the following for *each* of your quilt blocks:**

• Four 2⅜-inch light squares; cut each square in half *once* diagonally.

• One 2¾-inch light square; cut this square diagonally from corner to corner in *both* directions.

• Two 2⅜-inch dark squares; cut these squares in half *once* diagonally.

• One 2¾-inch medium square; cut this square diagonally from corner to corner in *both* directions.

Add visual interest by using a variety of values and small prints within the same Corner Cutter unit.

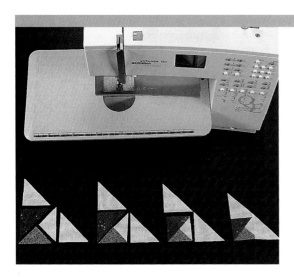

7

This Pinwheel design is directional, so take the time to lay out and piece the triangles in the correct sequence. Do this for each corner of each of your blocks. This step is well worth the extra time, to avoid Pinwheels that spin in different directions or blocks that don't form Pinwheels at all.

8

Center a Corner Cutter unit on each quilt block corner, with right sides facing, and trim the extending tips even with the quilt block. **Stitch the Corner Cutter unit in place.** Press the seam allowances toward the block to reduce bulk and help make the blocks lie flat. Don't expect to see the Pinwheel pattern emerging quite yet—that won't happen until you sew four blocks together.

9

Include Corner Cutter units in the border of a quilt to complete the Pinwheel designs at the outer edges of your blocks. Cut enough 3½-inch-wide border strips to frame your quilt; make sure that these strips are the same length as your framed blocks (*cut* size, not *finished* size). **Place the same Corner Cutter Guide at each end of the border strip, and trim away the corners so that the shapes that remain are trapezoids.**

Tip

Raid your collection of unfinished projects and see how many different types of blocks you can use in a quilt with Corner Cutters.

10

Sew a Corner Cutter unit to each end of your trimmed border strips. You will also need four Corner Squares. Cut two 3⅞-inch squares from the border fabric, and cut each in half diagonally. Stitch one of these triangles to a pieced Corner Cutter unit to make a Corner Square. **Arrange the quilt blocks, border strips, and Corner Squares, and double-check that all the Pinwheels "spin" in the same direction as in your blocks.** After checking all placements, finish assembling the quilt as you normally would.

The Quilter's
Problem Solver

Changing Gears!

Problem	Solution
You want to make Corner Cutter units that are larger or smaller than 3 inches, and don't know how to figure out what size to draw the Corner Cutter guide for your acrylic ruler.	To make any size Corner Cutter guide, always use graph paper that has 8 squares per inch. For the two short sides of a Corner Cutter guide, draw two lines to form a 90-degree angle, making each line exactly ⅛ inch longer than the finished Corner Cutter size you desire. Connect the open ends of the two lines to create the long side of the triangle.

You may end up with odd-size Pinwheel patches that can't be cut easily with a rotary ruler. In this case, you may wish to make and use templates, instead. Or consider a simpler Corner Cutter design. For example, divide the Corner Cutter triangle in half to create a two-piece Pinwheel unit, rather than the five-piece Pinwheel Corner Cutter shown in this chapter. Check out a reference book of quilt blocks for other blocks that can be divided in quarters diagonally. |

Skill Builder

"Reflect" on the possibilities: Design your own Corner Cutter units for framing strips.

On graph paper, draw a right triangle, and divide it into smaller patches, adding lines to create new designs. Stand two mirrors up along the two adjacent short sides, to preview how each design would look when repeated to form a square. Audition several more candidates for Corner Cutter units. Whether your design is symmetrical or asymmetrical, your mirror image could create some very interesting effects.

Try This!

Adapt the Corner Cutters technique to create specialty shapes, such as an octagon, or its pieced sister, the Snowball block.

For a 6-inch (finished-size) octagon, begin by cutting a 6½-inch square of fabric for the center. Then use a 2⅛-inch Corner Cutter guide to trim away the corners. To add contrasting triangles at the corners to make the Snowball block, cut two 2⅞-inch squares, and rotary cut them in half diagonally.

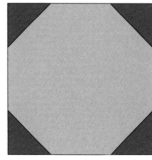

Snowball Block

Hand Piecing:
Perfect Points & Circles

For expert teacher Cindy Blackberg, there's nothing under the sun so enjoyable as hand piecing or hand picking a bouquet of flowers. For her, sunflowers are the perfect motifs for teaching students how to make sharp points and perfect circles. Cindy's special tricks come from the process of analyzing antique quilts and figuring out why some quilts do not lie flat. Her techniques will help you to acquire hand-piecing skills and make it one of your favorite pursuits.

Getting Ready

Make templates for hand piecing from heavy template plastic for durability. The translucent type makes it easy to trace a pattern underneath. Use a very fine-tip, permanent marking pen, which won't smear on template plastic.

A hard, nonslip surface is essential for accurately tracing around hand-piecing templates. Use a sandpaper board to keep fabrics from shifting around as you mark. Look for commercially available sandpaper boards at quilt shops, or make your own: Purchase fine-grit sandpaper at a hardware store, and use rubber cement to adhere it to a piece of heavy cardboard.

To produce thin, easily visible lines on fabric, use a regular pencil, or a Verithin yellow or silver pencil. Sharpen regular pencils often, to maintain consistency and accuracy when marking.

For visibility, contrasting thread is used in the photos in this chapter. For your own hand piecing, use threads that match your fabrics.

What You'll Need

- **Cotton fabrics**
- **Sandpaper board**
- **Template plastic**
- **Pencil or mechanical pencil**
- **Scissors for cutting template plastic**
- **Fine-tip, permanent marking pen**
- **Verithin yellow or silver pencil (optional)**
- **Fabric scissors**
- **Long, glass-headed straight pins**
- **Quilting thread to match fabrics**
- **Size 10 sharps (needles)**
- **Thimble (optional)**

Precision Points

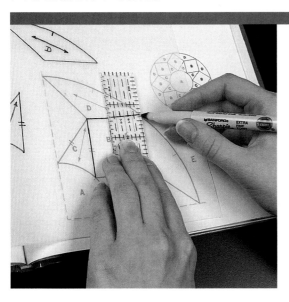

1

Using a fine-tip permanent marker, trace actual finished-size pattern pieces onto a piece of template plastic. For the Sunflower Quarter Pattern on page 47, trace A, B, C, and D pieces (or use another pattern you like). Include the letter of each piece, the grain line arrows to help you position the template on fabric, and all reference marks. Because there are no ¼-inch seam allowances included on templates for hand piecing, be sure to trace directly and accurately along the edges. When you cut out each template, cut *exactly* on the marked lines.

Tip

To trace circle A accurately, mark the dash lines, and align them carefully each time you rotate the pattern to complete the circle.

2

To mark patches accurately for hand piecing, place your fabric right side down on a sandpaper board. Position the templates with at least ¼ inch all around; align the arrows on templates with the fabric grain. Use a pencil that will provide good color contrast. Trace around the template, holding the pencil at an angle, rather than straight up, to keep your lines thin and precise. **At each corner, *extend* the pencil lines beyond the shape, to create accurate angles. Cut out each patch, adding ¼ inch outside the marked lines for seam allowances.**

Tip

To help match pieces accurately, add double hatch marks as reference points for joining two adjacent pieces.

3

After cutting out all of the patches for your project, **take the time to lay them out in the correct positions,** with either right or wrong sides consistently facing up. Analyze your layout carefully, to make sure that each of the patches is facing the right direction and is correctly positioned for your pattern. For any hand-piecing project, this is a good time to determine the most logical piecing sequence to follow.

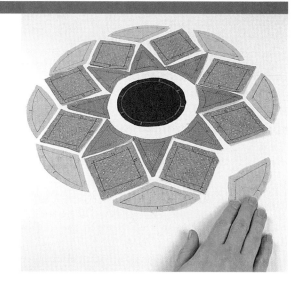

4

Pin a B patch on top of a C patch, with right sides together. Place a pin through both patches, *exactly* at the corners of the marked seam lines on both patches, *without* bringing the pins back up through the fabric. Place another pin through the middle of the seam line on both patches. **Instead of leaving the middle pin hanging, bring it back up through both layers of fabric, exactly on the marked line of both patches,** to secure the seam line for accurate hand piecing.

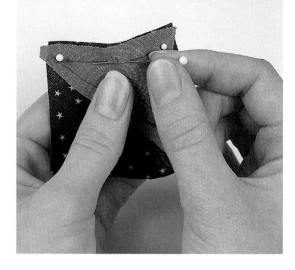

Tip

Sew with the lighter value fabric on top whenever possible, so you can see your marked seam lines better and stitch more accurately.

Thread a size 10 sharp needle with a 12-inch strand of thread, and knot the end. Insert the needle at the first corner pin, and remove the pin. Take one stitch, and backstitch to secure the knot. **Take tiny running stitches from this corner to the other, removing the middle pin when you reach it.** End your stitching by bringing the needle up exactly at the last pin, and taking two backstitches. Clip the thread, and replace the patches in your layout. **Continue until all B and C patches are joined as pairs.**

6

Pin two B and C units together with right sides facing as shown. **Pin each end of the seam line precisely, pushing the top seam allowance toward the right and the lower one toward the left,** so they are out of your way. Place another pin at the center of the seam line, matching up the pencil lines on both patches, as before. **Stitch this seam, beginning with the knot on top, taking one backstitch, and doing short running stitches.** End the seam precisely at the pin, take two backstitches, and clip the thread. Join all eight B and C units together in this way.

To inset a D patch, pin it to a B patch, right sides together, with a pin at the beginning and the end of the seam line, just before the B/C seam intersection. Begin at the outer edge and stitch the seam, bringing the needle up exactly at the pin. **Backstitch and insert the needle straight through the seam allowance between patches B and C.** You should still be on the top of your work. Align the next side of the D patch in the same way, take a backstitch after the seam allowance, and **continue stitching, ending with two backstitches as before.**

Tip

Instead of a neutral color thread, use one that matches either of the fabrics being joined, to avoid contrasting thread peeking out at seam intersections.

Tip

For greater accuracy and control, keep the piece or unit with the most seam allowances on top while you stitch.

HAND PIECING: PERFECT POINTS & CIRCLES

8

Fold the center circle (A) into eighths and finger-press these points along the edge. **With the Sunflower seam allowances facing you and right sides together, align the seams with creases on the A circle. Insert a pin just before each seam intersection.** Insert a threaded needle at the seam allowance, and backstitch. Taking one stitch at a time, **stitch from this seam line to the next,** checking the seam line on the circle as you go. At the first pin, backstitch, go straight through the seam allowance, take another backstitch, and continue stitching around the circle in the same way.

Tip

To center a circle shape on a background square, fold the background fabric in half in both directions and finger press quarter-circle reference marks.

9

Press the Sunflower unit from the wrong side, so it lies flat. To create a template for the circular opening in the background square, **turn your work over and use an acrylic ruler to measure through the center, *inside* the pencil lines.** Make a template of *this* size circle; the size may vary from the printed pattern, due to differences in stitching, thread, and pencil line widths. **Center the circle template on the wrong side of the background fabric, and trace around it.** Cut ¼ inch to the *inside* of the marked circle to create the seam allowance.

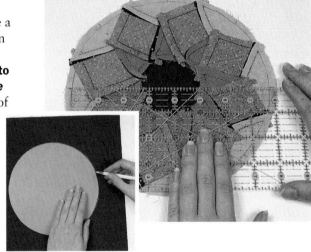

10

Crease the background fabric, dividing the circle into eighths. Pin the left side of each seam on the Sunflower unit to a crease on the background. **Stitch this circular seam as you did the small A center circle, backstitching at the point of each B patch.** Insert the needle through the seam allowance and backstitch on the other side of the point, piercing the previous backstitch. Backstitch again, tugging on the thread to make each point sharp. **Continue stitching to complete the block.**

The Quilter's
Problem Solver

Getting Right to the Point

Problem	Solution
You marked the fabric accurately, but somehow, your cut pieces do not line up when you pin them together for hand piecing.	Check to make sure that your pencil lines are not too thick. Whenever you mark around hand-piecing templates, make it a habit to sharpen your pencil often, so your lines will be thin and ensure accuracy. Whenever possible, sew with the lightest value fabric on top. This will make it easier to see your pencil lines and make your piecing more precise. It's also helpful to use a high-intensity lamp over your shoulder when hand piecing, to help you see your pencil lines better.
Your hand-pieced block looks ruffled and uneven around the outside edges.	Check the grain lines on the pattern, and make sure there are no bias cuts along the outside of the block. Replace patches as necessary, so that the outside edges of the block are either on the lengthwise or crosswise grain of the fabric.

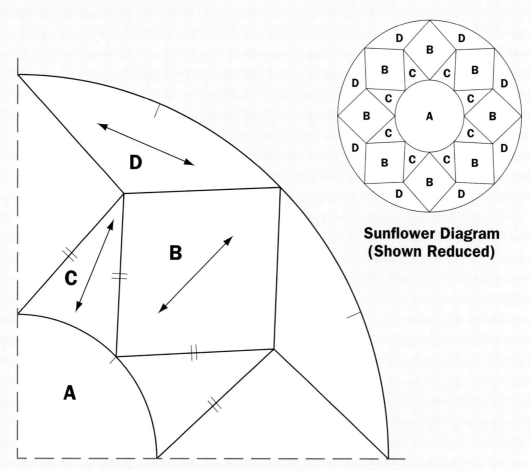

**Sunflower Diagram
(Shown Reduced)**

Quarter Pattern (Actual Size)

The Quilted Vest
at Its Best

Vests have always been a great choice for showcasing quilting in wearable form. The challenge is to look good—as both the maker and the wearer of a quilted vest. Beth Wheeler shares her ideas for a sophisticated, figure-flattering vest that will do you proud on both counts. A designer of dozens of vests for books and kits, Beth loves the way quilted vests dress up a basic outfit.

Getting Ready

Choose a commercial vest pattern, avoiding those with princess seams, darts, separate panels, or lots of pattern pieces. It's easy to alter the length, hem shape, and neckline of a simple pattern. You can also add pockets, closures, and other touches to create a whole wardrobe of different vests (see "Skill Builder" on page 53). Beth Wheeler uses the front and back pattern pieces to create the lining, and binds the edges as one would a quilt. Here, Beth uses Butterick pattern #5888, available in sizes 8 to 24, in the longer version without collar, pockets, or buttons and buttonholes. She places thin cotton batting only under the front sections, to provide gentle shaping and avoid bulk in back. If you want to make a thinner, cooler garment, consider using flannel, rather than batting.

Use a dark or quiet fabric for the back and background areas, and five fabrics in the same color but different values and print scales for the pieced areas. Place your fabrics side by side and experiment until you find a pleasing combination.

Take It from the Top!

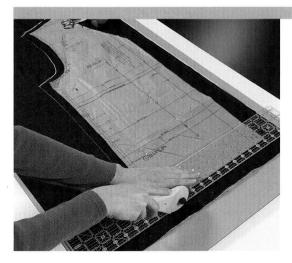

1

Cut out two vest fronts from the background fabric, cutting each one ¾ inch larger all around than the paper pattern, to allow for shrinkage during construction and quilting. Cut out two vest fronts from batting in the same manner. Use a rotary cutter, a long acrylic ruler, and a large cutting mat to cut the long, straight edges, and switch to scissors to cut the curves, "eyeballing" the extra ¾ inch as you cut. These pieces will be trimmed to size before you assemble the vest.

Tip

Move the fabric as needed to keep it over the cutting mat.

2

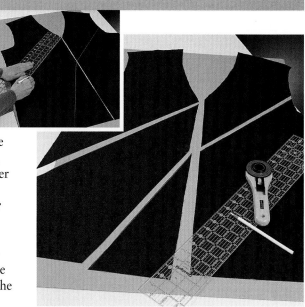

Mark diagonal lines on the right side of the vest fronts. Measure from your shoulder to waist and locate your waist point on each vest front opening, compensating for the extra margin of fabric at the shoulder. Mark from the waist to the center armhole on the left front. On the right front, mark from the waist out to the center of the bottom hem **and from the bottom of the neckline to the center of the side seam. Cut the fabric on these lines.** Remove the upper left section and center right sections; reserve the bottom right triangle to use later. Baste the remaining pieces to the batting fronts.

Tip

If you prefer a symmetrical design, mark one side, put the pieces together with right sides facing, and cut both layers at once.

3

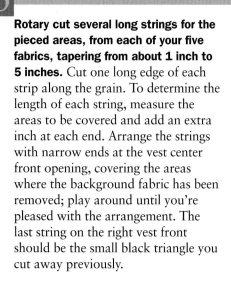

Rotary cut several long strings for the pieced areas, from each of your five fabrics, tapering from about 1 inch to 5 inches. Cut one long edge of each strip along the grain. To determine the length of each string, measure the areas to be covered and add an extra inch at each end. Arrange the strings with narrow ends at the vest center front opening, covering the areas where the background fabric has been removed; play around until you're pleased with the arrangement. The last string on the right vest front should be the small black triangle you cut away previously.

Tip

For continuity, use the same arrangement of fabric strings on both the left and right vest fronts.

4

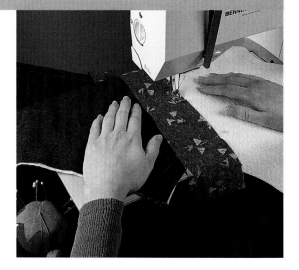

Place a prepared vest front right side up on a work surface. Pin the first string on the cut-away edge of the background fabric, with right side down, raw edges even, and an extra inch extending at both ends. Open up the string to ensure that once it's sewn and flipped over, it will cover the batting. **Stitch through the two layers of fabric and the layer of batting** with a ¼-inch seam allowance, to piece (and simultaneously quilt) the fabrics. Turn the string to its right side, and finger press it flat.

Tip

Wait until *after* finger pressing the strings open to trim the ends of strings even with the vest front edges.

5

Place a second string on top of the first one, with right sides together and the long, raw edges even. Pin and stitch the strings together along this edge. **Turn the top string to its right side, and finger press it flat.** Trim the excess fabric at both ends.

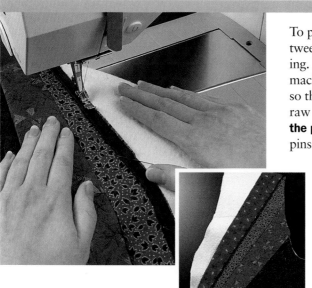

6

To provide some visual separation between strings in similar tones, add piping. Place a zipper foot on the sewing machine. Pin the piping along a string, so the raw-edged lip is even with the raw edge of the string. **Machine baste the piping close to the cord.** Remove pins as you reach them. Pin the next string over the same edge, right side down. Machine stitch from the batting side, guided by the basting stitches and keeping the needle snug against the cord of the piping; remove pins from the underside as you go. **Turn the top string to the right side, revealing the piping in between strips.**

Tip

As a variation to piping, you can insert prairie points in the seams.

7

Continue adding strings in the same manner, working toward the edges of the garment and covering the batting completely. **Repeat on the other vest front.** End with the small background-fabric triangle along the front opening. Working through the batting only (no backing), add decorative machine quilting to the vest fronts, and **free-motion quilt the background areas in stipple quilting.** (Refer to "Free-Motion Flourishes" on page 96.) Use a metallic or rayon thread in the top of the machine and regular sewing thread in the bobbin.

Tip

Try letting the print of the fabric inspire the lines of the decorative quilting stitches.

8

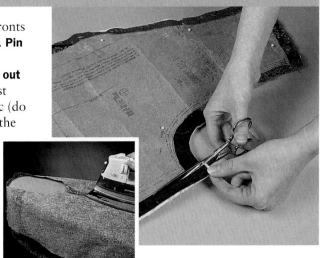

Press the string-pieced, quilted fronts with an iron, using a press cloth. **Pin the tissue pattern to each of the pieced vest fronts, and cut them out along the cutting lines.** Cut a vest back from the background fabric (do *not* add an extra ¾ inch). From the lining fabric, cut two vest fronts and a back using your purchased pattern. Pin the lining pieces together along the shoulders and side seams. Stitch, and **press the lining seam allowances open.**

Tip

Choose a favorite fabric for the lining; a neatly assembled vest will be reversible!

9

Sew the shoulder and side seams of the vest fronts and the vest back; press the seams open. Trim the batting close to the seam. Pin the vest shell and lining together with wrong sides together, matching shoulder and side seams. **Stitch around the outer edges with a ¾-inch seam allowance,** then trim the seam allowances to ¼ inch. Working from the right side, stitch in the ditch through the vest and lining along the shoulder and side seams, to prevent the lining from shifting. Use clear monofilament thread on top and thread that matches the lining in the bobbin.

10

Tip

Add embellishments such as beads or embroidery. Consider closures such as corded frogs or buttons and loops.

Bind all raw edges with binding strips, using ½-inch seam allowances. To make your own binding strips, **cut bias strips 2½ inches wide.** Stitch the ends together to create the needed lengths. Fold the binding in half lengthwise with wrong sides together, and press. Pin each folded binding strip to the vest shell, with right sides together and raw edges even, and stitch. Turn the folded edge to the lining side of the vest, and pin it in place just over the stitching line. **Slip stitch the folded edge to the lining.** Steam-press the finished vest.

The Quilter's
Problem Solver

Super Slenderizers!

Problem	Solution
How can you visually minimize a large bust?	Simplify the neckline of your vest by omitting collars or lapels.
What to do if you have large hips?	Adjust the pattern so your vest ends just above or just below the fullest part of the hips.
How about if you're large all over?	Do your strip or string piecing in vertical lines along the vest front openings, or shape bottom edges of the vest fronts so they are pointed, to emphasize vertical lines. Choose low-contrast fabrics (nothing cutesy).

Skill Builder

With one simple, basic vest pattern, you can create an entire wardrobe of gorgeous garments!

❏ Alter the neckline from V-shaped to round or square.

❏ Shorten or lengthen the vest pattern to a jaunty bolero or a calf-length duster.

❏ Change the bottom hemline from a square, boxy style to a rounded, bolero edge.

❏ Angle the bottom edges of the fronts asymmetrically.

❏ Add patch pockets, appliqués, epaulets, or plackets.

Try This!

Make a vest that incorporates fancy silks, laces, velvets, or rayons, in combination with quilter's cotton.

Stabilize slinky, fragile, or brittle fabrics with lightweight fusible interfacing before you begin. If your fabrics ravel easily, apply a bead of seam sealant to the cut edges and allow it to dry before strip piecing.

A delicate nineteenth-century rose quilt inspired Jeana Kimball's "Hexagon Rose" design. Stitching disconnected shapes, like the petals of this rose, is easy and accurate with her template-free appliqué technique. The only marking you'll need to do is on the wrong side of the background fabric. Jeana is happy to present her favorite appliqué technique, and you'll be thrilled with your stitched results!

Getting Ready

Template-free appliqué is great for individual nonlayered shapes, like the pattern in this chapter. Select fabrics in any color combination you like for your rose. Use coated, 100 percent cotton quilting thread, which will make basting, cutting, and removing stitches easier. For tracing appliqué shapes onto background fabric, you will need background light. Use a light box that is large enough to accommodate your entire pattern. If your project consists of very large blocks or units, tape your pattern to a window and let natural sunlight aid you, or make your own light box by laying a sheet of Plexiglas over an opened dining room table with one or two leaves removed. Place a table lamp underneath the Plexiglas, and you'll have a light box that will work well for any large design.

7½-inch square of background fabric

Assorted scraps of colorful prints for appliqué shapes

J.P. Coats or YLI coated, 100 percent cotton quilting thread in a light color

Threads to match appliqué fabrics

Light box (optional)

Long, straight pins with glass heads

Pencil

Straw needles (or milliner's needles): size 8 or 9, and size 10 or 11

Embroidery scissors

Masking tape (optional)

Preparing the Background Fabric

1

Trace the Hexagon Rose Appliqué Pattern from page 58 onto paper, and tape the paper on top of a light box with the marked side of the design down. This ensures that a finished design will be positioned correctly (an important factor with asymmetrical designs, unlike this one). Pin a square of background fabric right side down on top of the marked design. Using a pencil, **mark the entire appliqué design lightly on the wrong side of the background fabric.** This is the only time you need to mark your fabric—no templates will ever be needed. Take out the pins and remove the marked fabric and pattern from the light box.

2

Select the fabric that you want to use for the hexagon center of your rose. Cut a piece that is at least ¼ inch larger all around than the center piece of the appliqué design. Place it right side down on the light box. **Position the marked background fabric right side down on top.** The marked side of your background square should be facing up.

3

Use the light box to make sure that the background fabric is positioned correctly over your appliqué fabric. If necessary, adjust the background fabric over the appliqué fabric until approximately ¼ inch of the appliqué fabric extends beyond the lines of the drawn center piece on all sides. **Pin the two layered fabrics together, so that the points of the pins face outward and the shanks straddle the pencil line.**

Stitching the Appliqués

1

Using a size 8 or 9 straw needle threaded with a coated quilting thread, **baste the appliqué fabric for the center piece to the background square with short running stitches.** Work from the wrong side of the background square, and stitch exactly on the lines of the marked design. Leave approximately ¼-inch tails of thread at both ends of your stitching, and do not knot this basting thread, so that it will be easy to remove later.

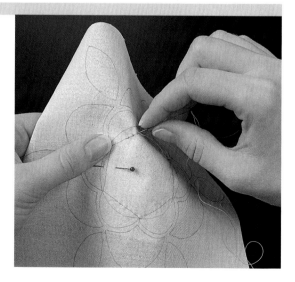

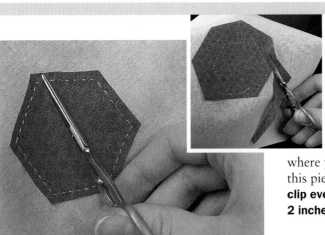

Working from the right side of the background square, **use a sharp pair of embroidery scissors to cut outside your basting stitches, leaving a scant ³⁄₁₆-inch seam allowance all around the shape.** At the point where you want to begin appliquéing this piece to the background fabric, **clip every other basting stitch for 1 to 2 inches.**

For making the most accurate cuts when doing hand appliqué, use a pair of embroidery scissors with a serrated edge on one of the blades.

3

Using a size 10 or 11 straw needle and thread to match the appliqué fabric, appliqué the center piece to the background square. **Start by positioning your needle between the raw edge of the appliqué shape and your basting stitches. Then gently scoop the fabric under with the point of your needle.**

Because the perforations left by your needle and quilting thread will have caused temporary indentations in the appliqué fabric, it will turn under easily. **Stitch the center piece in place on the background square,** cutting the basting threads 1 to 2 inches ahead of your stitching as you work your way around the piece. Turn your fabric over to the wrong side—**your stitches will match the marked lines of the design perfectly.**

TEMPLATE-FREE APPLIQUÉ

5

Stitch each of the remaining shapes in the rose design in the same manner. Press your finished block lightly from the wrong side.

**Hexagon Rose
Appliqué Pattern
(Actual Size)**

The Quilter's
Problem Solver

Follow the Dots for Perfect Stitches

Problem

With no marked lines to follow, stitching template-free appliqué shapes seems like it would be difficult.

Solution

Use the perforations left in an appliqué shape by the quilting thread to help you turn under seam allowances accurately. When you clip the basting threads and apply a bit of pressure to the seam allowance, these edges will automatically tend to fold. Match the perforations in your background fabric to the corresponding ones on an appliqué shape. These little holes tend to close up quickly, which is why it's a good idea to remove the basting threads just before you stitch the appliqué shape in place.

Learn to ignore the perforations in your appliqué shapes and background fabric altogether.

When you have become very comfortable doing template-free appliqué, try a slightly different approach. Pay attention to the design itself. In other words, allow your needle to help you "sculpt" individual shapes, making curves smoother and placing points where they will enhance the overall design, rather than following marked lines. This process is a lot like driving by watching the road ahead, rather than following lines painted on the highway.

Try This!

Catch up on clutter control!

Because template-free appliqué shapes are cut out as a design progresses (rather than all at once, before you begin stitching), it's easy to find yourself surrounded by large pieces of fabric for long periods of time. Try trimming away a smaller piece from the yardage of each appliqué fabric you plan to use and storing all of them in a plastic bag. You'll avoid annoying clutter, and it will be easier to work with smaller pieces of fabric.

TEMPLATE-FREE APPLIQUÉ

F lowers, foliage, and birds of many feathers flow through the colorful blocks in Suzanne Marshall's beautiful "Earth Watch" quilt. If at first glance complex units like these seem difficult to stitch, you're in for a pleasant surprise. Suzanne developed this unique method of hand appliqué that utilizes notebook paper to position shapes accurately. There's no need to use transparent overlays or mark the background fabric. Suzanne is partial to this technique because it makes the most intricate appliqué suddenly become simple!

Getting Ready

A flat work surface will make it easy to appliqué the design in this chapter. Keep your regular sewing supplies close at hand, and find a comfortable chair. Good lighting is a necessity, so sit by a window for natural light, or use a good lamp.

Lined notebook paper is an essential item for this technique. The lines are helpful for matching the grain lines in your appliqué shapes to the grain lines on your background fabric, making your appliqué look neat and consistent. Short extension lines make it easier to see how pieces relate to each other and to the background.

A bird pattern from Suzanne Marshall's quilt is provided on page 65 for learning the technique. If you'd like to create your own designs, a children's coloring book may provide great inspiration. Enlarge or reduce an image on a photocopier. Take time to figure out which shapes should overlap others, to determine the order of assembly before you start sewing.

Take It Away!

1

To create the background square, baste the 2½ × 6½-inch piece of green fabric across the lower portion of your background square, and hand appliqué it as shown. This will create the grass; the horizon between grass and sky will help you position your take-away appliqué bird. After stitching the grass strip in place, turn your work over, and trim the excess background fabric even with the seam allowance of your grass fabric.

TAKE-AWAY APPLIQUÉ

Tip

Look through books that contain appliqué patterns and practice figuring out the best stitching sequences for various patterns.

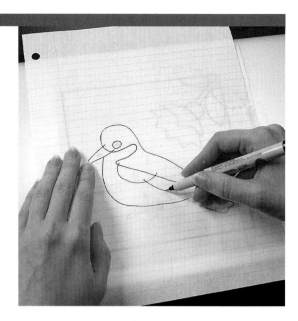

Photocopy the Bird Appliqué Pattern on page 65. Using a light box, trace the bird design onto a sheet of lined notebook paper, so that the lines on the notebook paper run horizontally across the design. Extend the lines of pieces in the design to make it easier to position each piece accurately in relation to the adjacent pieces. Number each piece in the design as shown, so that it will be easy to see the assembly sequence at a glance. To do take-away appliqué with other designs or patterns, determine which pieces overlap the others, and number them. This will show you the correct stitching order for your appliqué.

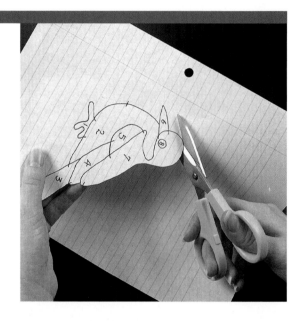

Cut out the notebook paper bird pattern. Use paper scissors, and cut along the outline of the bird only at this time. Turn the paper so that you are always cutting away from your body. You won't need to contort your wrist, and your cutting will be more precise.

Cut appliqué piece 1 (in this case, the foot) from the notebook paper pattern. Cut precisely on your drawn lines, so that the piece will be shaped correctly in your finished design.

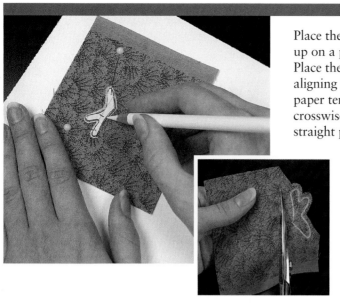

Place the fabric for the foot right side up on a piece of foamcore board. Place the paper foot pattern on top, aligning the lines of the notebook paper template with the lengthwise or crosswise grain of the fabric. Insert straight pins, anchoring the paper and fabric to the foamcore board. **Mark around the paper foot with a fabric-marking pencil.** Cut out the foot shape, adding a ³⁄₁₆-inch seam allowance, except where the foot will be over-lapped by the bird's body. **On this edge, add a ¼-inch seam allowance.**

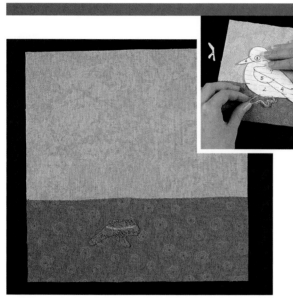

Place the notebook paper bird pattern on the back-ground square, matching up the horizon guidelines. **Slip the top of the fabric foot shape under the bird pattern, so that the marked lines on the foot match the extension lines on the body pattern.** The grain lines of all fabric pieces should be aligned with the hori-zontal lines on the notebook paper pattern. Pin the foot shape in place. **Appliqué it to the background square, working along all edges ex-cept the one that will be overlapped by the bird's body.**

TAKE-AWAY APPLIQUÉ

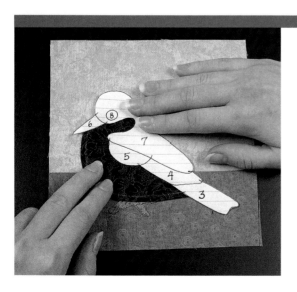

Cut piece 2 away from the notebook paper pattern, and use it to mark the bird's body shape on your fabric. Cut it out with a ³⁄₁₆-inch turn-under allowance around the lower curve and ¼ inch around the edges that will be overlapped by other shapes. Place the paper bird pattern on the background square, and **slip the fabric body shape under the paper pattern, and align it with the cut body shape, positioned in correct relation to the horizon.**

8

Pin the body in place and appliqué it to the background along the bottom curved edge, covering the top, raw edge of the foot. **Replace the paper pattern to check your work and to determine which will be the next "take away" piece.** (This assessment also allows you the opportunity to plan or rethink fabric choices for that next piece, in light of what's been done.)

9

Continue stitching successive pieces to the bird unit in the same manner, following the numbered sequence. **Each time you add another piece, reposition the remaining notebook pattern elements,** to be sure that the appliqué pieces are in the proper positions and to prepare for the next piece to be added.

10

After stitching the bird's eye in place, **compare your finished appliqué to the notebook paper bird pattern.** Make sure that no shapes are missing in the finished design.

 Tip

Check your button jar and choose a colorful button for the eye of this bird.

TAKE-AWAY APPLIQUÉ

11

You can use the same "take-away" method for adding shapes that go *beyond* the borders of a block, into a lattice strip or border. Appliqué the stem, flower, and lower leaf shapes at the upper right corner of the block in the same manner as you did for the bird, following the order numbered in green. Wait until after the quilt top has been assembled to appliqué the dashed lines of leaves 3 and 4.

Bird Appliqué Pattern
(Actual Size)

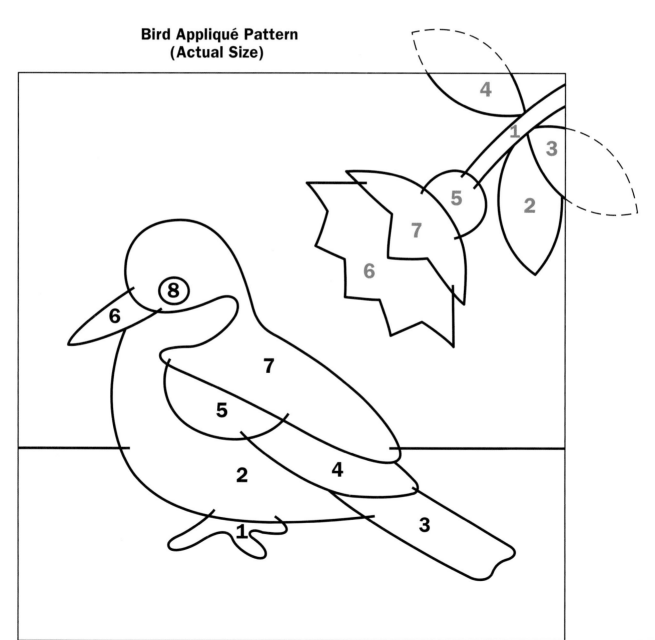

Cutwork
Lace

A Victorian lace collar inspired the delicate tracery of cutwork appliqué in "Linda's Lace," which has brought quilt artist Linda Pool a multitude of awards. Linda's technique for cutwork lace combines her love of appliqué with her passion for lace. Using just two fabrics, you, too, can create beautiful designs with an interplay of positive and negative spaces. Marking a pattern on a top layer of light fabric produces the positive visual image. Cutting inside the marked lines and stitching each shape to a lower layer of fabric reveals the background. Use Linda's original heart pattern to learn her pet version of reverse appliqué.

Getting Ready

For the top layer that will become your "lace," choose a light-color fabric, such as a white tone-on-tone print. Make sure that it's a finely woven cotton. Choose any contrasting color you like for the underneath layer or background fabric. For blocks, start with fabric squares that are larger than necessary, because appliqué will usually shrink the background slightly. For Linda's heart design, start with 8½-inch squares, and later trim the completed block to 8 inches square. For marking the heart design on freezer paper, use a black fine-tip permanent marker, so that the lines will not bleed. When marking your top layer of fabric, use a pencil and keep it sharp, so that your lines will be thin and easy to see. For best results while stitching cutwork lace, use Mettler size #60 machine embroidery thread.

What You'll Need

- **8½-inch squares of light-color fabric and contrasting fabric**
- **8-inch square of freezer paper**
- **Rotary cutting mat**
- **Square acrylic ruler**
- **Small utility knife (X-Acto)**
- **Fabric and paper scissors**
- **Embroidery scissors**
- **Black, fine-tip permanent marker**
- **Pencil**
- **Fine quilting or appliqué needle**
- **Mettler #60 machine embroidery thread (to match top fabric)**
- **Straight pins**
- **Thimble (optional)**

Preparing a Cutwork Pattern

1

Fold an 8-inch square of freezer paper in half, with the matte side up, and finger-crease it. Unfold the paper and center it, waxy side down, over the Heart Pattern on page 71 (or another cutwork pattern of your choice). Line up the crease with the short dashed lines at the top and bottom of Linda's pattern (or your own). **Using a fine-tip marker, trace the design to the right of the crease.** Linda's design is nearly symmetrical, except for a small, off-center highlight on the bow knot, shown on the pattern in purple. Trace this to the left of the crease in your freezer paper pattern.

2 Refold the freezer paper. Using an X-Acto knife or a small, sharp pair of paper scissors, cut a small slit through both layers of freezer paper inside each of the cutwork shapes; this will make it easier to cut out both shapes at the same time. **Using scissors, cut out each of the interior shapes** and cut around the outside edge of the design. Then unfold the freezer paper to cut out the bow knot highlight (or any asymmetrical elements in your pattern). **The freezer paper cut-out is now ready to use.**

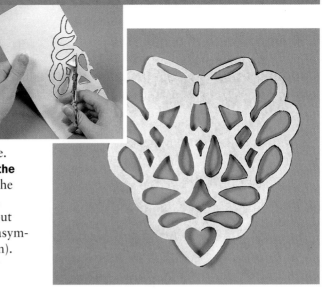

Tip

Place your top fabric on a piece of fine sandpaper before you mark, so it doesn't slip around.

3 Press the waxy side of the freezer paper cut-out onto the right side of a square of light-color fabric. This fabric will be used as the top layer for the reverse appliqué cutwork. **Using a sharp pencil, mark the complete design onto this top fabric.** To show the process clearly, marked lines here are heavier than they need to be. Press lightly; your lines should be thin, yet easily visible.

Tip

You may prefer to remove the freezer paper first, and cut slits inside the cutwork shapes with a sharp pair of embroidery scissors.

4 Place the marked top fabric on a cutting mat, **and use an X-Acto or a small utility knife to cut a ¼-inch slit in the center of each cutwork shape.** These slits will make it easy to insert the tip of your scissors when you begin to cut seam allowances. Be sure to cut *only* these short slits at this time, so that the fabric remains stable throughout the stitching process. Remove the freezer paper and save it for a future cutwork block.

5

Pin the marked top fabric to the background fabric, centering it carefully. Using thread just a little darker in color than your top fabric, **baste the marked design to the background fabric with short running stitches around each shape with a slit.**

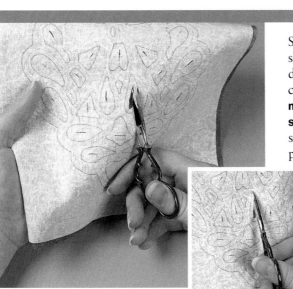

6

Starting at the center of the heart design, slip the point of your embroidery scissors into one of the slits you cut. **Cut the seam allowance approximately ⅛ to ³⁄₁₆ inch wide inside the shape.** In order to turn under this seam allowance easily as you appliqué it to the lower layer of fabric, you will need to make clips along the curves. Space these clips ⅛ to ¼ inch apart, depending on the depth of the curve. Sharper curves require closer clips than gentler ones. **At an inner point, clip right up to, but not through, your marked line.**

Tip

Cut out more than one shape at a time, if you like, as long as you appliqué all of them during the same sitting.

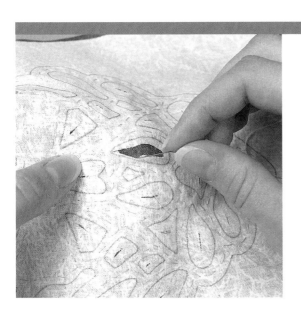

7

Thread your appliqué needle and bring it up from the wrong side of the background fabric, inside the reverse appliqué shape you want to stitch. **Use the tip of your needle to turn under the seam allowance,** starting ½ inch to the right of an inner point. When you can no longer see your marked pencil line, press the turned-under seam allowance with your left thumbnail, to keep it in position for stitching (reverse if you are left-handed).

Tip

Keep your needle almost flat against the fabric while you draw the seam allowance toward an inside point, to help sweep the fabric under smoothly.

CUTWORK LACE

8

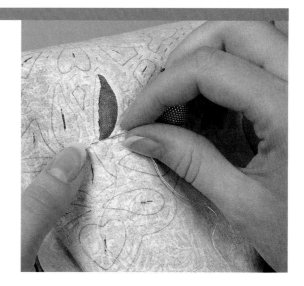

Start stitching the top fabric to the bottom fabric at the point where the thread comes out of the fabric, and **space your stitches approximately ¹⁄₁₆ to ⅛ inch apart as you work your way around the shape.** Stitch all of the remaining cutwork areas in the same manner.

9

After stitching each cutwork shape inside the heart, cut a ³⁄₁₆-inch seam allowance partway around the outline of the design. **Clip the seam allowances at the inner points and along the curves. Appliqué the outer edge of the heart shape to the bottom fabric,** one portion at a time. Remove the basting stitches after your stitching is complete.

10

Place the completed cutwork lace block face down on top of a padded surface, such as a terry cloth towel, and press it with a hot, dry iron. **Place the pressed block on a rotary cutting mat, and use a square acrylic ruler to trim the block to 8 inches.**

The Quilter's
Problem Solver

Improving & Moving Forward

Problem	Solution
You get points or peaks instead of smooth outer curves in your cutwork lace.	Stitches that are too far apart can cause peaks to form in an appliqué shape. Space your stitches close together and gently tug on the thread with each stitch you take, hiding it securely in the edge of the appliqué. Make sure you do not pull too tightly, however, which can make an edge look rippled.
You're inspired to design your own cutwork lace patterns. Where should you start?	Make a pattern from Battenburg lace by folding a piece of freezer paper in quarters, creasing the paper sharply. Use a pencil to draw curves and swirls from the lace onto one quarter of the paper. Simplify the design, and use a French curve to draw smooth shapes. Photocopy the design four times, and play with various arrangements of the copies. Enlarge or reduce your pattern as desired. Place folded freezer paper over one repeated section and trace it, following the directions in Step 1 on page 67.

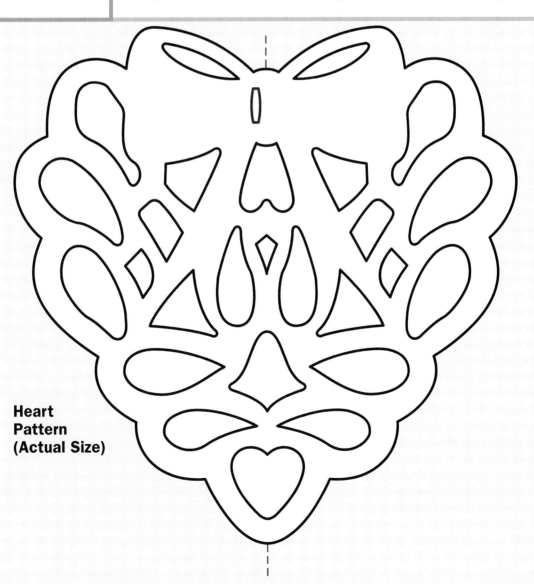

**Heart
Pattern
(Actual Size)**

Touches of Elegance:
Dimensional Flowers

S oftly scalloped flowers are luxurious accents in Anita Shackelford's "Flowers from
Friends" friendship album quilt. Anita's twentieth-century ways with this popular
nineteenth-century embellishment make it easy to stitch beautiful ruched blossoms and
buds. Her penchant for these dimensional flowers led her to develop her own marking and
gathering tool to create these classic roses. Follow her lead and let your next quilt bloom with
color and excitement.

Getting Ready

What You'll Need

7-inch square of fabric for flower

Background (or an appliqué block, ready for ruched flower)

Thread to match flower fabric

Fabric-marking pencil

RucheMark Circular Ruching Guide

Needle for hand stitching

Straight pins

Embroidery scissors

Small embroidery hoop (optional)

For best results in creating dimensional flowers, use a RucheMark Circular Ruching Guide—actually six guides on one sheet of heavy template plastic. (See "Resources" on page 126 for ordering information.) To make learning how to do ruched flowers easier, this chapter will lead you through fashioning the largest-size flower, which is 3 inches in diameter, plus a smaller bud. Check the chart below to determine which ruching guide to use for other flower sizes.

Choosing the Right Size Ruching Guide

Flower Size	Fabric	Ruching Guide
⅝"	2" square	#1
⅞"	2½" square	#2
1⅜"	4" square	#3
2"	5" square	#4
2½"	6" square	#5
3"	7" square	#6

Ruching a Full Rose

1

Select fabrics for your ruched flowers. Look for tone-on-tone prints that will produce both texture and shadows in finished roses. Use variegated fabrics that contain two colors for blossoms that have a two-tone look. Avoid using directional fabrics, such as stripes or plaids, which lose effectiveness when gathered. Also avoid busy prints on which markings will be hard to see.

2

Tape the background fabric on a flat surface and place the ruching guide on the right side of your fabric. **Mark a dot through each of the holes for the size flower you want, creating a zigzag pattern of dots in circular formation. Remove the ruching guide, and mark a line connecting the outer ring of dots to form a full circle.** This will be the turning line for the ruched flower. Cut out the circular motif, adding a ½-inch seam allowance outside your marked line, so that when you turn the fabric under, no raw edges will be visible around the outer edges of your flower.

3

Using thread to match the fabric, thread a needle and knot the end. Bring your needle up from the wrong side of the fabric at one of the dots on the outside line. **Turn under the raw edge of the fabric, and take three or four running stitches through both layers,** stopping at the next dot toward the center of the flower. Change direction, and take three or four more running stitches, working toward the outer edge of the flower. Bring the needle up at the next dot on the outer edge of the flower. **Gather your stitches; a petal forms between the stitched Vs.**

4

Continue taking running stitches around the entire flower, gathering them into petals as before. Do not backstitch or tie off your thread. Place the flower on your background fabric and spread the petals out, tightening or loosening your gathering thread as necessary, until the flower is the appropriate size and shape. Then knot and clip the thread on the wrong side of your work. Pin the ruched flower on your background fabric and **tack the outer edges in place, hiding one stitch behind each petal.**

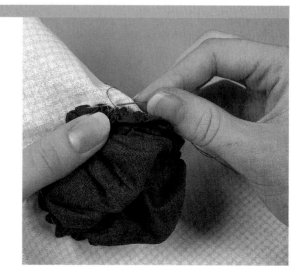

Ease the center fullness in place, and use as many tacking stitches as necessary to secure the "valleys" of fabric to the background. There is no need to work in any set pattern; simply tack enough so that the fullness is evenly distributed and creates a beautiful, textured center. For the purposes of visibility, contrasting white thread is shown here in place of matching thread.

Tip

Flatten out the puffiness with your thumb, then tack the "valleys" where they happen to fall.

Nipping-In a Bud

1

Choose a ruching guide two sizes smaller than your ruched flower. Mark dots around one half of this ruching guide on your bud fabric; add two extra dots to increase the bud's fullness. **Connect the outer ring of dots, as for the flower.** Cut across the unmarked portion, and follow the same stitching and gathering process as for the flower. Tuck the unstitched portion of the bud under a stem top and tack the petals and the center of the bud in place as you did before. **Then appliqué the edge of the stem top to the background fabric, over the flower bud.**

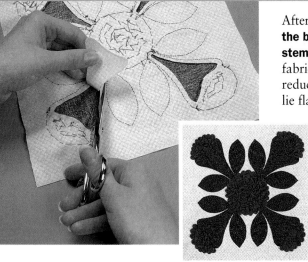

2

After your appliqué is finished, **cut the background fabric from behind the stem top.** Trim away any excess bud fabric from the wrong side. This will reduce bulk, and enable your piece to lie flat.

A Double Take on
Double Wedding Rings

A weaving exhibit that featured thick, textured pieces inspired Susan Stein to think up new ways to add visual interest to her favorite quilt pattern, the Double Wedding Ring. Inside-out patchwork seams and raw-edge appliqué put Susan's unique spin on this classic design. Decorative rayon seam tape is the icing on the "wedding" cake! Scope out your stash for colorful fabrics, and use Susan's techniques to create your own contemporary version of this—or any other—traditional quilt pattern.

Getting Ready

The more time you spend choosing fabrics, the more unique your Double Wedding Ring quilt will be. If you want the "rings" in your quilt to have a blended look, try using several gradations of a single color. Or mix different colors and experiment with the placements of light and dark values. Keep in mind that the wedge-shaped patches that make up the pieced rings should stand out from the background fabric.

The Plexiglas Double Wedding Ring templates from Quilting from the Heartland are great for rotary cutting curved patches quickly and accurately. Susan recommends putting self-adhesive sandpaper dots on the backs of these templates to prevent them from slipping; she also suggests using the smallest-size rotary cutter (28 mm) for best results when cutting small curved pieces.

What You'll Need

- **Double Wedding Ring templates and instructions**
- **Fabrics for pieced rings**
- **Fabrics for background, borders, and binding**
- **28 mm rotary cutter**
- **Rotary cutting mat**
- **Straight pins**
- **Sewing machine**
- **Coordinating color thread for piecing**
- **Chalk pencil**
- **Yardstick**
- **Rayon seam tape or silk ribbon for embellishing**
- **Any small, stiff-bristled brush**

Rings Around Tradition

1

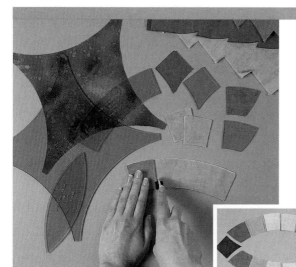

Using the Double Wedding Ring templates, **layer your fabrics and rotary cut as many wedges and background pieces as you need.** If you are using print fabrics, note that you will be sewing with wrong sides together, so the right sides of the fabric and the seam allowances will be visible on the surface (or right side) of the quilt. Susan Stein used hand-dyed fabrics for the rings in her quilt. If you work with solid or hand-dyed fabrics, you won't have to worry about right or wrong sides because they are identical. **Arrange the wedges for the pieced rings in the correct order before sewing.**

2

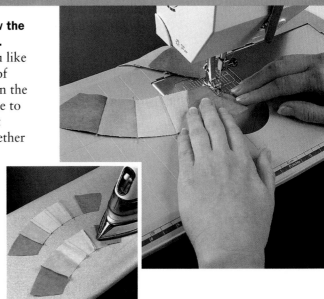

With wrong sides together, sew the wedge-shaped pieces into arcs. Choose a thread color that you like with your fabrics, because all of your stitching lines will show in the finished quilt. Set your machine to 8 to10 stitches per inch—short enough to hold the fabrics together securely, yet long enough for the line of thread to be a clearly noticeable design element. After piecing the arcs, **press them so that all seam allowances face the same direction.** Keep this direction consistent on all arcs.

3

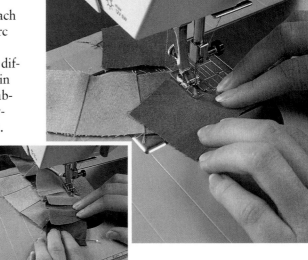

Sew a pressed arc to one side of each "melon" shape, with the pieced arc on top. **Sew a corner piece to the ends of each remaining arc,** using different colors at the two ends. Again sew with the wrong sides of the fabrics together. Press the seam allowances toward the center of the arc. Pin a pressed arc *with* corner pieces to the other side of each melon; match the seams and outside corners. **Sew the seam, attaching the arc to the melon and the corner pieces to the outside wedges of the opposite arc.** Press the seams toward the melons.

4

Tip

On your finished quilt, consider pressing the seam allowances randomly with an iron, for added surface texture.

Place your completed, pieced melons on an ironing board with the seam allowances facing up. Fix any seam allowances that may have become twisted, **and press the pieced melons gently.** Then turn the pieced melons over and press them again, from the other side.

To assemble the quilt, refer to your Double Wedding Ring instructions and arrange the large background pieces (which resemble squares with curved sides) and pieced melons into the required layout. **Sew pieced melons to the edges of the large background pieces.** Sew slowly and carefully so that your curves will be smooth and even. Remember, the stitches and seam allowances will show on the right side of the quilt top.

Tip

When piecing curves, always try to sew with the concave, or inner, curve on top.

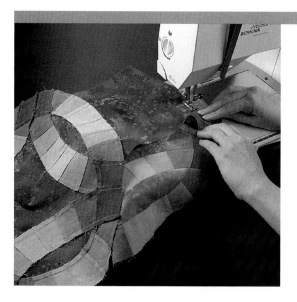

Stitch the pieced units and background pieces into rows, and then stitch the rows together, matching corner pieces. Add pieced arcs around the outer edges as necessary.

Cut border strips as needed for your quilt, allowing extra length for a mitered border. Lay these strips, centered, under your quilt top. Pin the pieced arcs in place so that they overlap the border strips by ¼ inch at the inner corners. At each corner, fold one border strip, so that it forms a 45-degree angle for the mitered corner seam. **Topstitch ¼ inch in from the raw outer edges of the rings.** Then miter the border corners and trim away the excess border fabric underneath the pieced arcs and the mitered corners, leaving ¼-inch seam allowances.

DOUBLE WEDDING RINGS

Tip

Consider hand painting or dyeing your own ribbon or tape to coordinate with the fabrics in your quilt.

8

Press your work; layer and baste the quilt top, batting, and backing. Give your Double Wedding Ring quilt added surface texture by stitching decorative trims on top. **Using a yardstick and a chalk pencil, draw several straight lines at random angles across the quilt top,** distributing these lines evenly. Lay silk ribbon or rayon seam tape over the marked lines, letting them extend past the edges of the quilt, and **straight stitch through the middle.** This will make the edges of the trim pop up, adding texture and shadows to the surface of your quilt.

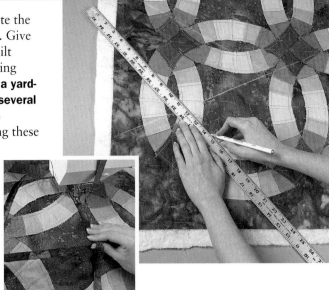

9

To add another element of interest to your quilt, cut out some leaves or other shapes for raw-edge appliqué. Position them on the corner squares of the melons with a glue stick. **Put a darning foot on your sewing machine, and topstitch ⅛ inch in from the edges of your appliqué motifs.** Since you are working through several layers, you will be machine quilting the leaves at the same time you are applying them. Use a slightly shorter stitch length this time, to hold the edges securely.

10

Quilt by hand or machine. Bind your quilt, making sure to capture the ends of the rayon seam tape or ribbon in the binding. Then shake your quilt and **brush the raw edges to fray the fabrics attractively.**

Go for the Unexpected!

Problem	Solution
Your quilt looks too predictable, even though you used exciting designer fabrics and hand-dyes.	Visible seam allowances and raw-edge appliqué are just the beginning! Here are some other ideas to consider: ❏ Lay colorful strands of yarn in front of your presser foot. Couch them to a quilt with nylon thread and a narrow zigzag stitch. ❏ Adhere craft foil to the surface. Look for these iron-on metallic embellishments at craft and quilting stores. ❏ Tack silk ribbon on the quilt with decorative hand stitching or beading. ❏ Make three-dimensional flowers and vines, and sew them to the quilt surface.

Skill Builder

One block—nine lives!

Experiment with texturizing techniques, by making nine blocks, all using the same patchwork pattern and fabrics. Do something different with each block—add raw-edge piecing to one, add a ribbon overlay to one, paint areas of another, adorn still another with buttons, sequins, or trinkets. Continue adding any embellishments you can think up, keeping them to one color family so that your finished blocks will look unified. Arrange them into a Nine-Patch setting with sashings and borders.

Try This!

Use fabric you no longer like for some coloring experiments.

Try painting over the fabric with textile paint that blends in with your print, and tones down and enhances what is already there. Stuff some fabric into a resealable plastic bag and pour dye over it. Seal the bag and turn it upside down repeatedly. As the dye settles into the wrinkles and folds of the fabric, interesting patterns will result.

Celebrate the new century by using two different retro needlework and craft techniques together for a fresh, updated look. Noted quilt teacher Jill Sutton Filo shows you how to embellish fabric with crayon craft, which was popular in the 1920s and 1930s. She likes to emphasize the design lines using traditional redwork embroidery, a passion of American quilters since the 1880s. Try out this unique combination of Jill's favorite techniques, and create designs on fabric that will serve as charming focal points for your next quilt project.

Getting Ready

Sources of inspiration for crayon craft and redwork designs—used separately or together—are virtually everywhere. Scour craft magazines, children's story books, and coloring books for simple line drawings and motifs. For crayon craft, you can use either regular children's crayons or fabric crayons. Regular crayons offer a huge range of colors and produce vivid results; however, they may gradually fade after each washing. If you plan to launder your project repeatedly (such as a child's wearable), use fabric crayons and follow the manufacturer's instructions (which require different methods than those in this chapter). By itself or combined with crayon craft, redwork is wonderful for a limitless variety of projects, from pillows and quilts to purses, country-style vests to jackets and baby bibs, and more. Choose medium or dark red floss for a classic look.

What You'll Need

- **Simple floral design**
- **Prewashed, light-color fabric**
- **Fabric-marking pencil or mechanical pencil**
- **Light box (optional)**
- **Crayons**
- **Paper towels**
- **Iron and ironing surface**
- **Embroidery hoop**
- **Red and green six-strand embroidery floss**
- **Embroidery needle**
- **Embroidery scissors**

Crayon Craft

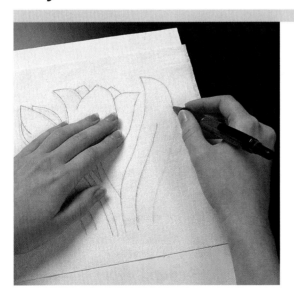

1

Trace the Tulip Pattern on page 123 onto light-color fabric, using a fabric-marking or mechanical pencil. Or, select another simple design that has fairly large, easy-to-color shapes for crayon craft. If necessary, use a light box or a sunny window to trace the design.

Tip

After tracing a design onto fabric, press freezer paper to the wrong side, to stiffen it for easier coloring. Remove the paper before you embroider.

2

Using crayons, color in your design. Blend colors as you would in a painting. Move gradually from dark to light, or add an accent color, such as purple or blue, along the edges of the design.

3

Place a paper towel over your ironing board cover to protect it. **Place the colored design right side down on top of the paper towel, and press the wrong side of the fabric with a hot, dry iron.** The color will bleed through the fabric slightly as the crayon melts and bonds with the fabric, so you can see what's been ironed. Move the iron slowly back and forth, so that you do not scorch the fabric. After pressing, the colors will seem brighter and the coloring lines will look softer.

Redwork

1

Place your fabric in an embroidery hoop. Cut an 18- to 20-inch length of red floss. Use two strands for a delicate look, or three for a bolder look. Leave a 3-inch tail on the wrong side of the fabric, and begin doing the stem stitch (see page 122). Start away from a corner or the center of a line, so that your stitches will flow smoothly. **Keep your stitch length, angle, and tension consistent, and keep the floss consistently either above or below your sewing line.** This will help you maintain even tension, and keep the floss out of your stitching path.

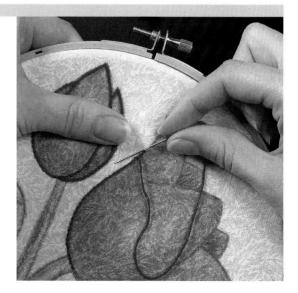

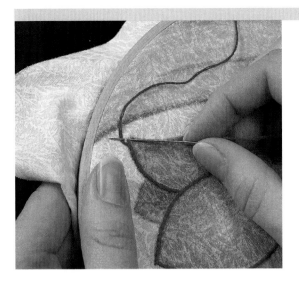

When you come to a point, such as the tip of a leaf or flower petal, try this trick: Make a very small stitch at the end of your line of stitches, so that you can bring the needle out of the fabric close to the corner. **To turn the corner, insert your needle into the fabric *near* the corner, but *on* the adjacent sewing line. Bring the point of the needle out of the fabric just a scant ¹⁄₁₆ inch beyond the corner, with the thread under the needle.** When you pull the needle through, this stitch will jut out slightly.

Tip

For smoother, prettier stitches, let your needle dangle occasionally to untwist the strands of floss so they will lie side by side.

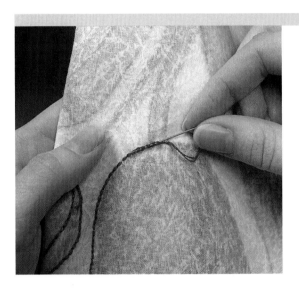

3

To end a length of floss, bring your needle to the wrong side of the fabric and weave the floss through your previous few stitches for about ½ inch. Weave the tail at the beginning through a few stitches in the same way. Trim the excess, leaving no more than ⅛ inch of floss. To start a new length of floss along the same design line, rethread the needle and weave the floss through your previous stitches for about ½ inch, then continue stitching. Your thread ends will be neat and secure on the wrong side of your work.

Tip

Use other decorative stitches, such as buttonhole stitching, chain stitching, or cross-stitch, as accents and borders around crayoned designs.

For a refreshing, new approach, try blue, brown, green, or even purple floss! **You may wish to use green embroidery floss to embroider around the stem and leaves, in the same manner as for the redwork flower heads.** After finishing your embroidery, press your work from the wrong side. Again, place a paper towel underneath to protect your ironing board cover from any crayon residue. Now it is ready to incorporate into a project.

Tip

Wash soiled redwork projects (with or without crayon craft) separately. Use lukewarm water with a mild detergent or dishwashing liquid.

REVIVAL TECHNIQUES

Fun with Sun Printing

Although Diane Bartels has mastered printing on fabric using her computer, scanner, and printer, she willingly forgoes such high-tech processes for the exciting surprises and sheer delight of sun printing. With this technique, Diane picks her designs right off the trees. Besides leaves, all that's required are light-sensitive paints, cloth, and a sunny day. Unbelievably easy to do, each sun print is one of a kind, and will make any quilt unique.

Getting Ready

Wait for a hot, sunny, windless day for the best sun-printing results. The stronger the sun, the crisper your sun-printed images will be. Choose a shady spot in which to apply the paint. You'll need to work quickly, so find a large enough work surface to keep all of your materials close at hand. Either cut or tear your fabric into manageable sizes. Spread a large plastic drop cloth, a shower curtain liner, or a tarp in an area that receives full sun, where your painted prints are to dry.

Setacolor Transparent paints are "helio-tropic," which means that their pigments intensify under the sun. These paints come in about 20 different colors; very dark and bright colors will produce the most dramatic sun prints. Purchase a few 45-milliliter jars, and mix your own colors. The paints will go far because you dilute them with lots of water. Refer to "Resources" on page 126 for ordering information.

What You'll Need

- **Prewashed and pressed white cotton fabric**
- **Pressed leaves**
- **Pebeo's Setacolor Transparent paints, two or more colors**
- **Foam brushes**
- **Wide-mouth jars or bowls**
- **Flat tray or board**
- **Jar of water**
- **Paper towels**
- **Plastic drop cloth**
- **Rubber gloves**
- **Small stones (optional)**

Playing with Paint & Leaves

At least a day before you plan to print, go outside and pick some leaves. **Choose leaves or groups of leaves with interesting outlines.** Press the leaves between layers of news-paper and weight the top with a board or heavy books. It's important to have leaves that will lie very flat when you get to the actual process of printing.

Tip

Press plenty of leaves. While you can occasionally use a leaf more than once, don't count on it.

2

Mix different paints in wide-mouth
containers to obtain the colors you
want. **Experiment with small dabs of
color.** Whether you mix paint colors
or use the color as it is straight from
the jar, dilute paints with water,
combining *at least* two parts water
to one part paint. Make up small
amounts (⅛ or ¼ cup) of diluted
paint to pour into a bowl or pan, so
you can reach the paint with a foam
brush. Have a jar of water handy for
rinsing brushes.

3

Begin at your table in the shade.
**Working quickly, apply paint to your
fabric.** You don't want the paint to
dry until you can move it into an
area that receives full sunlight. Use
one color or blend different colors on
the fabric, completely saturating and
covering the surface.

4

Lay a leaf on the painted fabric on
top of a tray or board. **Press the leaf
down with your fingers so that it lies
completely flat and makes complete
contact with the painted cloth.**
Place your work on the plastic drop
cloth on the ground. Place small
stones on the leaf to hold it down in
case of a sudden breeze. Then let
the sun do its work. In a very short
time—usually 10 to 20 minutes—the
fabric will be dry and the sun print
will be finished.

5

Lift the leaf up from the surface of the dried fabric. (In some cases, the leaf will have adhered to the paint, and you may have to peel it off in pieces. In other cases, the leaf may now be too crinkly to lie flat for a second sun print.) **Where the sun has shone directly on the fabric, the color will be fairly intense. Where the leaf has masked the fabric, the color will be much paler.**

6

Heat-set your sun print by one of these methods: (a) Place the print *paint side down* over a paper towel on an ironing surface. **Press with a dry iron on a cotton setting** (or a temperature appropriate for the type of fabric you are using). (b) Place the sun print in the dryer on a regular setting for 45 minutes. (c) Preheat the oven to 210°F, then turn it off. Lay the fabric on aluminum foil and put it in the warm oven for about 10 minutes. After heat-setting the color, wash, dry, and press the fabric. Your sun print is now permanent and ready to use.

Variations on a Theme

Feeling adventurous? Explore the effects you'll get from using different fabrics. Instead of plain white fabric, **use solid colors, quiet prints, or hand-dyed fabrics.** Paint the fabric and lay a leaf on it as before. The original color or pattern of the fabric will show up a little better where the leaf masks the fabric under it.

Tip

Instead of leaves, use pressed flowers, sea shells, feathers, paper doilies, or bathtub decals to make sun prints!

FUN WITH SUN PRINTING

89

Good Marks
for Quilted Borders

An exquisitely quilted border frames the pastel Whig's Defeat blocks in Elsie
Campbell's quilt, "Aunt Mimi's Triumph." Marking border designs, especially on a
large quilt, can be a daunting task. Elsie developed her own method using freezer
paper. She loves this technique because she can mark borders of any size or shape—from
miniature to bed-size—easily and accurately. And no matter whether the quilt is square or
rectangular, with straight or scalloped edges, the borders turn out perfect every time.

Getting Ready

You can use almost any type of quilting design when you mark borders with this technique. As you choose a quilting design for the borders of a quilt, consider incorporating design elements from the center of the quilt or echoing motifs from your fabrics in the quilted borders. Appliqué and patchwork patterns, magazines, and books are good sources of design inspiration. The more time and thought you put into choosing quilting designs for the borders, the more unified and interesting your finished quilt will look. For help in marking large borders, you might consider transforming your dining room table into a light table as described in "Try This!" on page 95.

"Try This!" on page 95.

What You'll Need

- **Completed quilt top**
- **120-inch tape measure**
- **Freezer paper**
- **Mechanical pencil**
- **Eraser**
- **Light box**
- **Black permanent, felt-tip marker**
- **12-inch square acrylic ruler with 45-degree angle marks**
- **Iron and ironing surface**
- **Fabric-marking pens or pencils**
- **Glass-headed straight pins (optional)**
- **French curve (optional)**

Bordering Square Quilts

Measure all sides of the finished quilt top (a square quilt may not be perfectly square), and write down these measurements. Cut a piece of freezer paper to the exact length of one half of the finished border. Trim the freezer paper border to the width of the finished border. Mark the corner area, and fold the rest of the paper into as many repeats as needed or desired for your quilting design. Mark the repeat lines along the creases, using a pencil and ruler. **Add a line ½ inch in from the outer edge to allow for any trimming or squaring up that may be necessary after quilting.**

Tip

For a scalloped border, mark and cut the freezer paper to match the scalloped outer edges of the quilt.

Sketch or trace your quilting design lightly in pencil inside the first repeat. Adapt and adjust the design as necessary to fill the space nicely. Darken the lines of your finished design by tracing over it with a black permanent, felt-tip marker. With the shiny sides together, fold the freezer paper on the next repeat line, and trace the design in the next space with the black marker. Use a light box to make the tracing process easier. Continue marking repeats until you reach the corner area.

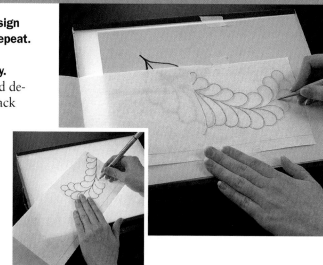

Use your 12-inch acrylic square ruler and a pencil to mark a diagonal line through the corner of the freezer paper border, so it will start at the corner of the quilt top and extend to the outer corner of the border. Fold the freezer paper border so you can trace the design from the previous repeat onto one half of the corner, stopping at the marked diagonal line. Open the freezer paper border and adjust the center of the design to fill this half of the corner area attractively. Use French curves from art or office supply stores to aid in drawing smooth curves.

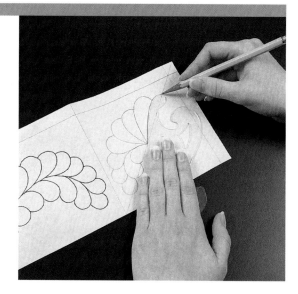

Tip

Fill in empty areas between design repeats with small motifs, such as hearts, posies, or leaves.

Go over the lines with the black marker. Refold the corner along the diagonal line. Use the black marker to trace the quilting design onto the unmarked half of the corner. Unfold the finished corner.

Cut a second freezer paper border the same length as half of your finished border *without* the corner, and add an extra inch for an overlap. Place the second freezer paper border at a right angle to the first, with the matte sides up and the marked corner overlapping the second border by 1 inch. Using an acrylic square ruler, check to make sure that these borders form a perfect 90-degree angle. **Press the freezer paper together at the overlap with a hot, dry iron,** and allow the paper to cool; the freezer paper borders will be well bonded.

Fold the joined freezer paper borders along the diagonal line at the corner, with the shiny sides together, matching the edges of the borders. **Using a light box and black permanent marker, trace the quilting design onto the unmarked freezer paper border.**

Lay your quilt top, wrong side up, on an ironing surface. Place the freezer paper border on top, with the marked side facing up; align it with a corner and two adjacent sides of your quilt. If necessary, insert glass-headed straight pins through the freezer paper border, the outer edges of the quilt, and into the ironing surface, to keep the weight of the quilt top from pulling it off the ironing surface. **Using a dry iron on the cotton setting, press the entire freezer paper border in place.**

Tip

For pressing large quilt tops, you may want to invest in a Big Board, which will greatly increase the surface of your ironing board.

Tip

Don't use a water-soluble marking pen! Ironing the freezer paper border onto adjacent areas could permanently set the lines you have already marked.

When the freezer paper and fabric have cooled, **place the quilt right side up on a large flat surface, and trace the quilting design onto the right side of your quilt with a fabric-marking pencil or mechanical pencil.** If your chosen fabric makes the markings hard to see and trace, use the light box again.

Tip

To make minor adjustments, simply lift the freezer paper border and reposition it, making sure the lines of your quilting design meet.

Carefully remove the freezer paper border from your quilt top, and reposition and press it onto the next quarter of your quilt top. Mark the quilting design in this section of the border. Because you cut the freezer paper border to the same size as your quilt border and marked the design by folding one side of the paper over the other, the lines of your quilting design should meet each other perfectly as you work your way around the entire quilt.

Bordering Rectangular Quilts

Cut a freezer paper pattern to the size of one long border, including both corners. Cut two pieces of freezer paper to the finished width and half the length of the shorter borders, *without* the corners; add 1 inch for overlap. Draft and mark the repeats and corner, folding and tracing as necessary to complete the patterns. Press the short pattern pieces to opposite ends of the long one to bond, completing a half-pattern for the entire quilt border. Press it to the wrong side of half of your quilt border. **Mark the quilting design on the fabric.** Remove the freezer paper, reposition it on the other half, and complete the marking.

Marks & Re-Marks

Problem	Solution
You want to add background lines to your quilting design, but using freezer paper patterns prevents you from attaining consistent line directions.	Wait to mark any straight lines or other background quilting lines until *after* you have marked more elaborate quilting motifs with the freezer paper method. Use a ruler or other straight edge to make sure that your straight lines match, and mark directly on the quilt top. You can even wait until after you have quilted the elaborate designs, and then use quilter's masking tape to mark straight lines.
A silver pencil does not show up well on dark fabric or busy prints.	Use a Nonce white pencil. The marks will stay on fabric for up to 2 years, and they can be removed easily with a damp cloth. This pencil is soft enough to mark without a lot of drag. Keep a little pencil sharpener handy, so that you can maintain a fine point on your pencils throughout the entire marking process.

Skill Builder

Let your border design "travel" all the way around the quilt.

To make a continuous quilting design, cut a piece of paper exactly the size of one repeat in your quilt border. Trace the quilting design in this section and darken the lines. Position this pattern repeat under a freezer paper master pattern folded into repeats, and trace the design continuously from section to section. Take care in aligning the motifs in each repeat, and make any necessary adjustments at the corners, to ensure that the quilting design will flow well around the quilt. When you are satisfied with the marked design, darken all lines on the freezer paper master pattern.

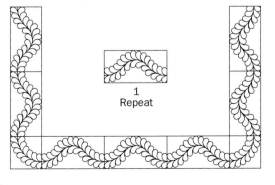

1
Repeat

Try This!

Make a large light table for marking large quilts!

Remove a leaf or two from your dining room table and lay a large piece of Plexiglas across the opening. Place a table lamp, minus its shade, under the table, and turn it on. Position a bed-size quilt over your newly made light table—you'll love being able to mark large portions of a quilt without frequent repositionings.

GOOD MARKS FOR QUILTED BORDERS

Free-Motion
Flourishes

After commissioning a stained glass window for her quilt shop, Laura Heine decided to interpret the same design in fabric using her favorite stitching techniques and threads. In her resulting "Spool of Thread" quilt, she encrusted flower petals and leaves with her signature free-motion stitching, then outlined the shapes in black. Laura loves to enrich and even change the look of a quilt design with thread. She also added dimension with "faux" trapunto, another machine technique.

Getting Ready

Any fused appliqué block or quilt top with simple shapes will work for free-motion embroidery techniques. Use lightweight fusible web that bonds well and is designed for stitching, such as WonderUnder or Steam-a-Seam II. Set up your sewing machine for free-motion stitching: Lower the feed dogs, put on a darning foot, and loosen the top tension slightly. Practice on test swatches of similar-weight fabric and fusible appliqués. First, stitch several straight lines by manually controlling the movement of the fabric. Adjust the tension as needed. Continue to practice stitching, moving the fabric in all directions and striving for a consistent stitch length. Next, set the machine for zigzag stitches and try stitching as you move the fabric. Also, practice stipple quilting, working over batting and backing. This methodical preparation will help you gain control and enjoy the freedom of free-motion stitching

What You'll Need

Flower fused on a 12½-inch square of background fabric

½ yard of lightweight fusible web

Darning foot

Size 90/14 machine embroidery needle

8- to 10-inch wooden embroidery hoop

Decorative threads: YLI Ultrasheen or Sulky Rayon for machine embroidery

Black cotton thread

Two 14-inch squares of thin cotton batting

Blunt-tipped scissors

YLI Washaway and Jean Stitch black thread

14-inch square of backing fabric

Thread for machine quilting

Size #1 safety pins

Embellishing with Thread

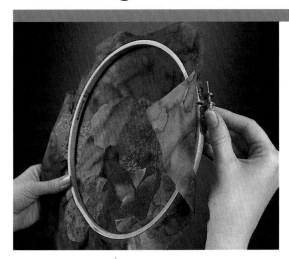

1

Place a fused floral appliqué block (or quilt top) in a machine embroidery hoop with the screw closure on the wrong side of the block or quilt top. Your work should be flush with your sewing machine surface when it is underneath the presser foot. Tighten the hoop until your block is as tight as a drum.

2

Put a darning foot, or another foot
designed for free-motion embroidery,
on your machine. Wind black cotton
thread on the bobbin and use YLI
Ultrasheen or Sulky Rayon decorative
thread on top. Set your machine for
straight stitching. Move the hoop and
**free-motion stitch in generous zigzags
around the edges of the appliqués on
your block,** securing the fused edges
to the background fabric. Make some
lines of stitching long and others
short for an interesting look. Make
sure that your stitches stay on the
fused shape and do not wander onto
the background area.

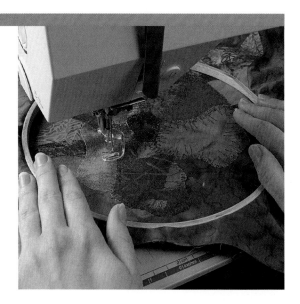

3

To fill in each flower petal with
overall texture, change to a zigzag
stitch. Play around on a piece of
scrap fabric until you determine the
width you like. **Cover each flower
petal with uneven zigzag stitching,
moving the fabric back and forth,
working in an area about ½ inch
square.** Avoid making your stitching
too dense; the fabric should show
through your zigzag. Stay inside the
edges of the fused petal.

4

Try stitching some free-motion leaves
and vines in a continuous pattern.
Set your machine to a straight stitch,
and start at an edge of the appliqué
shape. Outline a ½-inch heart-
shaped leaf, starting and ending at
the base of the leaf. Stitch about
halfway into the center of the leaf,
creating a vein, and return to the
base of the leaf. Stitch a vine that
curves around the completed leaf,
and then move on to free-motion
stitch another leaf in the adjacent
space. **Fill in the entire area, ending
with a vein.**

After you have covered the fused design with decorative stitching, remove it from the hoop and layer your block on top of lightweight cotton batting that is cut 1 inch larger than your block all around. This layer of batting will add dimension to the flower, giving it the look of trapunto. **Pin the block and batting together with several size #1 nickel-plated safety pins.** Place the pins only in the areas outside of the appliqué.

Tip

Be sure to use nickel-plated safety pins to baste the layers of a quilt sandwich together, to avoid problems with rust on your fabric.

Change to YLI Washaway basting thread in the top of your machine; keep cotton thread in the bobbin. You will be removing the Washaway basting thread with water later, after all quilting is finished. **Free-motion stitch the block to the batting along the outer edges of the appliqués, sewing in a continuous stitching line.** There is no need to completely stitch around each petal and leaf—just go around the outside edges of the appliqués. Remove the safety pins when your stitches get close to them.

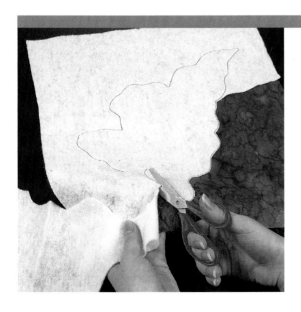

Using a pair of scissors with blunt tips, trim away the excess batting as close to your stitching line as possible. Take care not to cut through your stitches or the background fabric. The batting under the appliqués will create the trapunto look. If you accidentally cut through your block when trimming away the batting, fuse a small piece of Steam-a-Seam II over the cut area on the wrong side. Tear the paper away, and fuse a small piece of the background fabric to the side of the fusible web that is exposed.

8

Cut a piece of batting and background fabric, each at least 1 inch larger all around than your block. Place the background fabric wrong side up, and layer the batting on top. Center your block over the batting. **Pin this layered quilt sandwich together at approximately 1½-inch intervals, using size #1 nickel-plated safety pins.** Place the pins in the trapuntoed areas, as well as over the rest of the block.

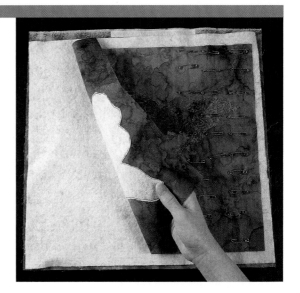

Tip

Mentally plot a course for your stippling so it fills areas nicely rather than runs in monotonous rows.

9

Using YLI Ultrasheen or Sulky Rayon thread, free-motion stipple quilt the background area, stitching right up to the edges of the appliqués. Keep your stipple stitches fairly small, so that the background is densely quilted and the trapuntoed areas puff out nicely by contrast. Remove the safety pins from the background area as you reach them.

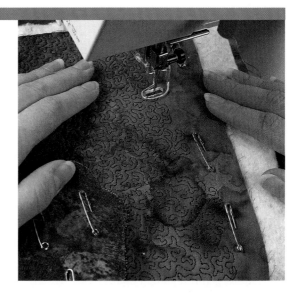

10

Change to a heavy, black thread, such as YLI Jean Stitch thread, in the top of your machine. Use black cotton thread in the bobbin. **Free-motion stitch around each of the appliqués to outline them boldly.** This will create dramatic black outlines that define the trapuntoed areas. For a thicker outline, stitch around each shape two times. Plan your stitching to avoid cutting the thread as much as possible. Strive for a continuous line around the entire design. When all quilting is done, immerse the quilt in tepid water to remove the water-soluble thread.

The Quilter's
Problem Solver

Thick Thread Woes

Problem	Solution
My machine does not "like" Jean Stitch thread. I have problems with tension and the fabric becomes puckered.	Try slightly loosening the tension on the top of your sewing machine. Using a size 90/14 machine embroidery needle will usually help, too. Be sure your bobbin is in the bobbin case correctly (refer to your sewing machine manual if you are unsure). If you are still having trouble, you may need to change to a needle with a larger eye, such as a size 100 Jeans Denim needle. Closely woven fabrics sometimes require this kind of needle to allow the thread to pass through the eye easily.

Skill Builder

Think up other interesting designs to free-motion embroider inside appliqué shapes.

Once you start down this path, you may never want to turn back! The sky's the limit—try using different types of threads and an array of beautiful colors inside one flower shape, and let your imagination take over from there, as you add color contrast and texture to flowers and leaves.

Try This!

Tighten the upper tension on your sewing machine slightly, so that you pull the black thread from the bobbin more to the surface of your block or quilt top.

Use this trick to add interesting shading to your machine embroidery. It may look funny when you start, as if your tension is adjusted incorrectly. But when you finish stitching, the black threads all come together and your design will look great!

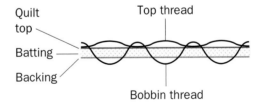

Quilt top — Top thread
Batting
Backing — Bobbin thread

FREE-MOTION FLOURISHES

101

Taming
the Embellished Quilt

Quilt artist Mary Stori is well-known for quilts that are filled with wit, whimsy, and charm. Her favorite technique is embellishing with festive charms, trinkets, found items, and often weighty three-dimensional accents. This can wreak havoc with a quilt that you want to hang straight and flat. Mary's simple construction system will allow you to stabilize an embellished quilt, add trouble-free borders, and include built-in margins for error. Your finished quilts will hang straight and true.

Getting Ready

Quilts embellished with dimensional appliqué, embroidery, beads, trinkets, or other found objects can often become uneven because the extra stitching required to add these embellishments causes the quilt to draw in, distort, or develop rippled edges. In addition, unevenly distributed embellishments can cause stretching or distortion, if they are plentiful or heavy. In the steps that follow, Mary Stori shares her technique for stabilizing the background prior to embellishing, and then adding borders. Take accurate measurements as you construct the quilt, and work on the largest flat surface you can find. An ideal work table is about 72 inches long and 36 inches wide, but you can also put several smaller tables together to form one large surface, or work on the floor if that is comfortable for you.

What You'll Need

Appliqué pattern *or* completed quilt top center

Muslin, washed and pressed for appliquéd and pieced backgrounds

80/20 cotton/poly batting

Beads, ribbons, and trinkets

Thread to match fabrics

Tape measure

6 × 24-inch and 6½- or 12½-inch square acrylic rulers

Rotary cutter and mat

Iron and ironing surface

Straight pins

Removable marking pencil

Pencil

Sewing machine

Walking foot

Stabilizing Pieced or Appliquéd Backgrounds

Before adding borders or embellishments, **appliqué the background for your embellished wall quilt directly onto a muslin foundation.** To do this, determine the size of your finished quilt top, including the seam allowances (without borders). Add ¼ inch on all four sides and cut a piece of muslin to this size. As you appliqué pieces onto the muslin background, add ¼ inch to each piece that lies at an outside edge. This extra ¼ inch will act as a margin for error, allowing you to square up the quilt center before adding the borders. Press the completed background.

2

If you plan to machine quilt, you'll need to add all dimensional embellishments afterward. However, if you plan to hand quilt, complete the quilt top and add the embellishments *before* you quilt, stitching or tacking through the muslin foundation. Then, **in areas where there are no embellishments, trim away portions of the muslin foundation from behind the appliquéd background.** Avoid a lot of hand quilting around the embellishments, where you'll still have an extra layer of fabric to stitch through.

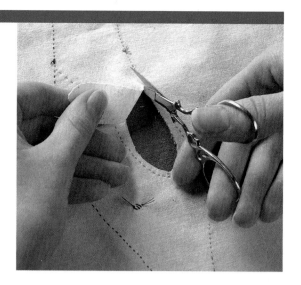

Stabilizing Whole-Cloth Backgrounds

Quilts with a single background layer also benefit from stabilizing. The best foundation is an 80 percent cotton/20 percent polyester batting because these strong fibers eliminate the need for a layer of muslin. Cut both the batting and the prepared whole-cloth fabric ¼ inch larger than required, to create a margin for error. **Place the batting under the quilt top and generously thread-baste the two layers together,** working from the center outward and stitching horizontally and vertically in a grid, and all around the edges.

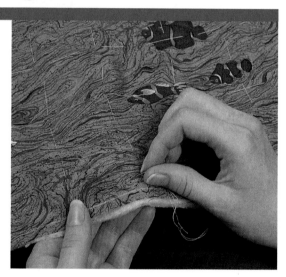

Embellishments

1

Maximize the benefit of using a foundation under an embellished quilt. Treat the two layers as one as you appliqué additional designs, embroider, add beads, or incorporate other embellishments. **Balance the distribution of heavy objects evenly over the quilt top.**

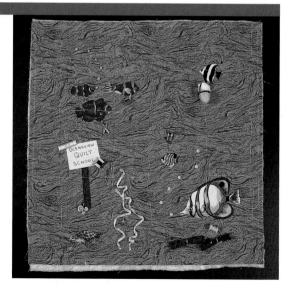

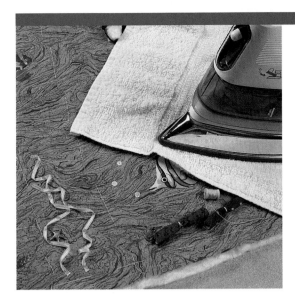

After your design is completed, you should press the quilt top as flat as possible. Work with the quilt top facing up to prevent damage to the embellishments. Do not iron areas with heavy or thick embellishments. For other areas, **cover with a slightly damp terry cloth towel and press.**

3

Lay the quilt on a cutting surface to straighten the edges. To maintain 90-degree corners, place a square acrylic ruler on your quilt, so that the fabric you need to trim lies outside the ruler's right edge and the top of the quilt is parallel to the lines on the ruler. Place a narrow acrylic ruler along the edge of the quilt, aligning the short end with the square ruler. **Trim away the excess fabric to create a straight, even edge.** Repeat on all sides of the quilt, squaring from the side you've already trimmed.

Tip

For embellishments near the corners or edges of a quilt, use a combination of smaller acrylic rulers so they will lie flatter as you trim.

Heading for the Borders

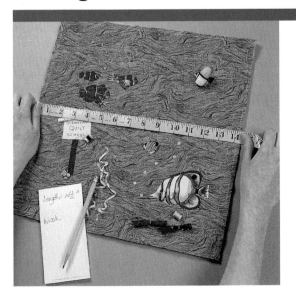

Determine the accurate border dimensions for your quilt by taking measurements through the center of the trimmed quilt top. For quilts that are wider or longer than the length of your ruler, or quilts that are heavily embellished, use a tape measure. First, measure the length, down the center of the quilt top, from the top raw edge to the bottom raw edge. Jot down these dimensions on a piece of paper. **For the width, measure from side to side through the center, raw edge to raw edge, and write down these dimensions.**

2

Decide how wide you want the finished borders to be, and add ½ inch for seam allowances *plus* an extra ¼ inch as a margin for error. This will allow you to trim the borders of your finished quilt straight and true.

Determine the length of the border strips as follows: For the top and bottom border strips, use the width measurement from Step 1. For the side border strips, use the length measurement from Step 1, plus two times the finished width of the borders, plus ½ inch for seam allowances, plus an extra ¼ inch as a margin for error.

3

Tip

To help the fabrics "bond" and prevent them from shifting during sewing, lightly steam-press them together.

Mark the center of each side border strip and the center point on each edge of the quilt top. Pin the borders and the quilt top right sides together, matching these points (keeping any batting out of the way). **Sew the top and bottom borders to the quilt top, using a walking foot and a ¼-inch seam allowance.** Repeat for the side borders. If you have used batting as the stabilizer, cut corresponding strips from batting and place them behind the attached borders, **joining them to the batting at the back of the quilt with whipstitches.** Layer, baste, and quilt your quilt.

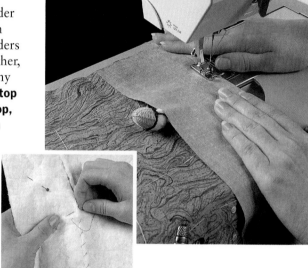

4

After you finish quilting, lay your quilt on a flat surface and examine the borders. Trim uneven or rippled edges. To adjust and maintain 90-degree corners, place a square acrylic ruler on the top of the quilt, so that the fabric you need to trim lies outside the ruler's edge, and the top edge aligns with the quilt top. Lay a long acrylic ruler on top of the side border, and align the two rulers. **Using a rotary cutter, trim away the excess fabric in the border to achieve a straight edge.** Repeat on all four sides. Bind the quilt, adding a hanging sleeve at the top edge.

The Quilter's
Problem Solver

Ripples, Waves & Weighty Problems

Problem	Solution
The edges of the embellished quilt center are ripply and wavy after squaring up.	Before adding borders, baste around the outer edges. Pull the basting stitches slightly to help control the ripples and waves. The measurements of the sides should equal the measurements that you took through the center.
Your quilt is large, with a lot of embellishments in the bottom portion.	Put a hanging sleeve at the bottom of the quilt, as well as at the top, to hold the lower edge straight and even and to help support the weight of the embellishments in that area.

Skill Builder

Attach odd-shaped embellishments with beads.

Make a thread loop strung with beads for the item to hang from. Treat any item with holes like a button; come up from the wrong side, through one of the holes, and add as many beads as necessary to span the distance between the holes. Then pass down into the second hole and fabric. Tie off on the wrong side. Match the thread to the embellishment item whenever possible, and use strong thread such as Nymo Beading Thread, Coats and Clark Hand Quilting Thread, or silk thread.

Try This!

Visit a craft or dollhouse miniatures store.

You may find the perfect embellishments for your next quilt. Look for these and other items that you can attach to a quilt with tacking stitches.

- ❑ Wooden spools
- ❑ Sequins, beads, and other sparkly trinkets
- ❑ Charms
- ❑ Decorative buttons
- ❑ Diminutive dolls
- ❑ Tiny sewing machine
- ❑ Faux jewelry
- ❑ Miniature-scale fabrics, in bundles or packets
- ❑ Doll garments
- ❑ Flowers
- ❑ Small pieces of dollhouse furniture

Quilt Repairs
Made Easy

I f the quilt you rescued from the trunk in your Grandmother's attic has a gaping hole in the fabric, or the sails on the sailboat quilt your child drags around with him have ripped, don't despair! Unmistakable signs of age or excessive wear needn't be causes for alarm. Eileen Trestain, a noted authority, teacher, and long-time collector of vintage and antique quilts, offers her favorite techniques and shows you how to remedy the situation.

Getting Ready

Before you attempt any repair, first ask these questions: Is the quilt connected to a momentous event in history? A famous person? Is it a rare find from before 1850? If the answer to any of these is yes, this quilt should be handled only by a reputable, professional conservator. This chapter will give you guidance on quilts, new or old, that have sentimental or other value, but are not so historical or precious that they would decrease in value from any restorative efforts.

The most common repair is replacing worn or damaged fabric in individual patches or larger areas of the front or backing. When fragments of the original fabrics remain, use them as guides for choosing good replacement fabrics in the appropriate colors and designs. For an older quilt, look for good replacement fabrics with a textile or antique quilt dealer. Take along a color photocopy of the fabric you want to replace. For both new and old quilts, there are beautiful reproduction fabrics to choose from.

What You'll Need

Vintage or reproduction fabrics

Safety pins; silk pins

8½ × 11-inch self-adhesive label paper

Size 10 or 11 milliner's needles

Cotton quilting thread

White fabric or nonwoven interfacing

White cotton sewing thread

Tailor's chalk or mechanical pencil

Fabric scissors

Silk or cotton machine embroidery thread to match replacement fabrics

Dye, such as Rit liquid dye (optional)

Synthrapol (optional)

Bridal Illusion or fine tulle

Replacing Patches

Insert a safety pin at each damaged spot to identify all of the areas in a quilt where fabric needs to be replaced. The number of pins will be a visual clue as to the quilt's condition, and will give you an idea of how much work needs to be done to repair it.

Tip

Inspect a silk quilt closely for needed repairs, but avoid handling it excessively or using safety pins, which leave large holes in the delicate fabric.

2

To replace a single patch, **make a
template of the shape you need by
photocopying the damaged area onto
an 8½ × 11-inch sheet of self-
adhesive label paper.** Do the same
for every patch you need to replace
in the quilt. Cut out the photocopied
template. Peel off the backing from
the label paper, and adhere
it to your replacement
fabric, matching the grain.
**Cut the replacement patch
¼ inch larger on all sides
than the template, for seam
allowances.**

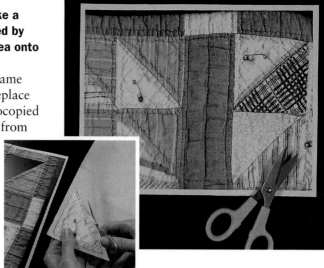

3

As you prepare to repair each damaged area, remove the safety pins and
leave the damaged fabric in the quilt.
Align the replacement patch, with the
template still in place, over the damaged area. **Pin the patch in position,
using silk pins.** Insert the pins only
through the seam allowance of the replacement patch and into the top
layer of the quilt.

4

**Using a milliner's needle, appliqué the
replacement patch over the damaged
area.** Avoid catching the batting and
backing layers in your stitching. After
you have finished stitching, peel off
the self-adhesive template from the
patch. Without using a hoop (which
could distort or damage the fabric),
**requilt the patch you have
replaced, using quilting
thread that closely matches
the original thread used in
the quilt.** Also, match the
length of your stitches and
the spaces between them as
much as possible to the
original quilting stitches.

Creating Replacement Fabric

Need to repair an area but can't find a fabric that closely matches it? If the area is light colored, you can easily make your own replacement fabric. Start with a color photocopy of the fabric to be replaced. Purchase solid-color fabric in the color and weight you need for your replacement fabric. **Place this fabric over the photocopy, using a light box if necessary, and trace the design of the original fabric with textile pens.** Use a hot iron to heat-set the pigments so they are permanent.

Make a photo transfer of an elaborate fabric print that you can't match. Refer to "Making Memories" on page 114.

Repairing Holes

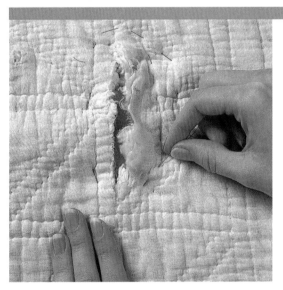

1

You *can* repair a hole that goes through all three layers of a quilt. To start, cut a piece of white fabric (or nonwoven, nonfusible interfacing) at least 1 inch larger than the hole. Working from the top side of the quilt, pin the white fabric over the hole. Carefully turn the quilt over so that the backing is facing up. Make sure the area around the hole is not stretched or distorted. **Stabilize the damaged area of the quilt by basting through all layers,** especially around the area of the hole, securing the white fabric or interfacing in place. Then remove the pins.

2

Select a replacement fabric that matches the backing of the quilt. Following quilting lines or seam lines on the quilt whenever possible, **use a piece of tailor's chalk or a pencil to carefully sketch the outline of the area to be repaired on a piece of the replacement fabric.** Add a ¼-inch seam allowance all around. Using a pencil on light fabrics and tailor's chalk on dark fabrics will make it easy to remove your drawn lines if you need to adjust the size of the piece to fit the space.

Make sure that you align the grain lines of the patch with those of the backing fabric, especially for light-color replacement fabrics.

QUILT REPAIRS MADE EASY

3

Cut out the marked piece of replacement fabric and pin it over the hole in the quilt backing with silk pins. **Appliqué it in place,** removing pins as you come to them. After you finish stitching, turn the quilt over, take out the basting stitches, and remove the white fabric from the right side of the quilt.

4

Choose batting with a loft and fiber content similar to the original batt. Cut a piece to fit the damaged area. **Baste the replacement batting to the edges of the batting in the quilt.** Use white cotton thread (black thread is shown here for visibility). Avoid stitching through to the backing. Repair the right side of the quilt top as in "Replacing Patches" on page 109. Using cotton quilting thread that matches the original thread, requilt the repaired area, matching the stitch length of the original quilting stitches.

Beyond Repair?

Tip

A pair of appliqué scissors, with a broad, blunt, bottom blade is great for the delicate job of trimming only a top layer.

The market value of a very old quilt will decrease with repairs. To preserve a quilt and slow its deterioration, stabilize and protect it with sheer fabric. Bridal Illusion and tulle are inexpensive, available in several colors, and will not ravel. Cut a piece of sheer fabric about 1 inch larger than the area you want to preserve. Place it over the damaged area and take ¼-inch-long running stitches through the sheer fabric, working along the seams in the damaged area. **Carefully trim away the excess sheer fabric, leaving about ⅛ inch beyond your stitching for security.**

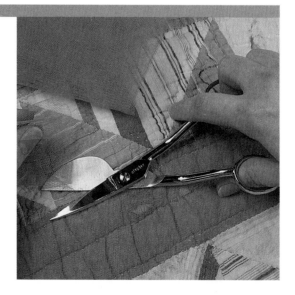

The Quilter's
Problem Solver

Cleaning Challenges

Problem	Solution
You don't know whether or how to clean an antique quilt.	Evaluate each antique quilt on its own merits. While some are strong enough to be cleaned, many are not. Older quilts can also contain fugitive dyes, which can bleed and damage the quilt. Do not dry clean a vintage quilt. For laundering advice, consult an experienced quilt appraiser, a quilt restoration specialist, or a museum curator, who can guide you in achieving the best possible results for your quilt.
You want to save an antique quilt that is infested with insects.	Seal the quilt tightly in a large, plastic garbage bag, and put it in a freezer for three days. Remove the quilt, handling it carefully to avoid breaking the frozen fibers. Allow the quilt to come to room temperature. After three more days, refreeze it in the same manner, to kill any possible hatchlings. After thawing it again, cover the end of a vacuum cleaner hose with a nylon stocking or fiberglass screen, and vacuum the entire surface of the quilt, front and back. This treatment is also effective in reducing the musty smell of mildew. Freezing a quilt in a plastic bag is also helpful for preserving a quilt that has been in a flood, until you can clean it.

Skill Builder

Use silk crepeline to preserve a badly damaged quilt for historical reasons.

For areas where only the warp or weft threads remain intact, insert a matching piece of replacement fabric underneath the threads (use tweezers to lift the threads, if necessary). Smooth the threads over the replacement fabric in parallel lines, and couch them in place with an overcast stitch. Appliqué silk crepeline over the repaired area, to preserve the threads and keep them from continuing to wear. Silk crepeline comes in white or brown; if necessary, dye it with Rit liquid dye to match your quilt. Consult a trained conservator before attempting crepeline preservation on valuable quilts.

Try This!

If you have a collection of antique quilts or have a family heirloom quilt that you know you will want to keep in good shape, build up a special stash for repairs.

Start a collection of reproduction and vintage fabrics, buying appropriate fabrics whenever you spot them. Similarly, when you make a new quilt, bundle up the leftover fabrics so you'll have a repair kit for the future. Keep them in a labeled cloth bag or a mesh laundry bag. Wash these fabric pieces whenever the quilt is washed so they'll always look the same.

Making Memories:
Family Album Quilts

L et quiltmaking expert and author Ami Simms show you how she created her "Family Fotos" quilt with photo transfers. Ami finds these quilts very satisfying to make, because they allow her to relive the past and ponder the future. The photographs freeze time, and using photographic images in fiber adds a compelling dimension unlike any other. You'll find yourself wanting to create a magnificent memory quilt of your own, incorporating photographs of family members, friends, and special occasions. And you'll discover how easy it is to do!

Getting Ready

Since photo transfers are not opaque, the color of the fabric you use will show through the transfer. (Avoid green fabrics, which will make the people in your photo transfer look seasick!) For best color reproduction, use bright white, 100 percent cotton fabric, such as Springmaid Southern Belle. The smoother the fabric you use (200-thread count is the ultimate), the better your transfer results will be. If possible, use unwashed fabric, because the sizing gives the surface shine and crispness—the perfect background for photo transfers.

You can transfer cherished family pictures easily, without harming them in any way. You can also use flat or fairly flat objects that are small enough to fit on the bed of a color photocopy machine: children's art, ticket stubs, letters, jewelry, and other mementoes. For best results, use Photos-To-Fabric transfer paper (see "Resources" on page 126).

What You'll Need

Clear, sharp photographs (or other flat objects)

8½ × 11-inch plain, white paper

Scotch removable double-coated tape

Color photocopy machine

Photos-To-Fabric transfer paper

Paper scissors

Unwashed, 200-thread count, white cotton fabric

Rotary cutting supplies

Iron

Photo Transfer

1

Select the photos you want to transfer to fabric, keeping in mind that the best pictures also make the best photo transfers. **Choose snapshots that are properly exposed and well focused. Under- or over-exposed, or out-of-focus photos will not improve when they are transferred to fabric.** Also, make sure that the subject takes up most of the space in your photo. If necessary, you can crop the image and remove extraneous background areas, but it's best to start with a clear image that is large enough to see easily.

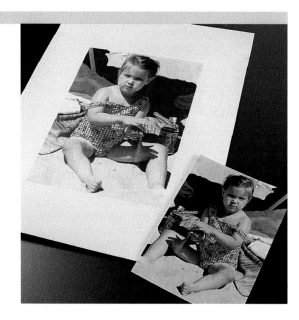

2

Depending on the space you have, you may want (or need) to enlarge or reduce a photograph to fit. Since the final image will be the mirror image of your photo, you may also want to reverse the original image. You can do all of this easily with the push of a button or two on a color photocopy machine. **Work with the original and enlarge, reduce, or produce a mirror image when you make the color copy onto the transfer paper.** Make the photo transfer directly from the original photo, not from a color photocopy. Images lose clarity with each generation they are removed from the original.

Tip

Reducing an image makes it harder to see a picture's shortcomings, but enlarging more than 175 percent can produce grainy, dull transfers.

3

Get the most out of one sheet of photo transfer paper: **Tape several photographs you want to transfer to fabric on a piece of plain, white paper, using removable double-coated tape.** Butt the images edge to edge, and leave a ¼-inch margin around the edges of the paper, because photocopy machines will not print in these areas. Overlap the photos to save space or mask portions of pictures that you do not wish to include in a transferred image.

Tip

Use photo transfers to personalize quilt labels.

4

Take your prepared layout of photos, along with Photos-To-Fabric transfer paper and instructions, to a place where there is a color photocopy machine, such as a large office supply store or quick printing business. Call ahead to see if someone experienced in making color copies onto transfer paper can help you. Ask for a color copy on regular paper first, to make sure that colors are true to your original images. Then ask for a mirror image of your originals to be made on the transfer paper. **The transfer paper image will be backward, but the final transferred image will read correctly.**

Tip

Have the technician increase the brightness when printing on the photo-transfer paper, as the image tends to darken slightly when ironed.

Cut out the first image you want to transfer from the sheet of transfer paper, taking care to trim very close to the image. Press your unwashed white fabric to remove any wrinkles, and check to be sure that both the photo transfer paper and the white fabric are free of dust or stray fibers, which can cause permanent blemishes in the finished photo transfer.

Tip

Avoid placing photos over hard creases, like the center fold of your fabric, which is nearly impossible to flatten. Work around them, instead.

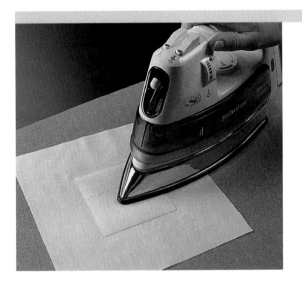

Place a transfer paper photo face down on the right side of your white fabric, aligning the photo edges with the grain of the fabric and leaving margins of at least ¼ inch, for seam allowances. Plan for even larger margins if you want white fabric to show around the image. **Press for 30 seconds with a dry iron on the cotton setting.** The more pressure you put on the iron, the better results you will have in the transferred image. Slide the iron back and forth as you press, so that the steam vents do not remain in the same place for very long.

Tip

If you scorch the transfer paper or your white fabric, reduce the amount of time you press, or the temperature of your iron, or both, on your next attempt.

After you have pressed the image onto the fabric for 30 seconds, remove the iron and **peel off the paper while it is still hot.** Start at a corner. If the paper does not come off easily, simply reheat it with the iron for 5 to 10 seconds and try again.

Tip

Inspect the transfer as you peel. If it is incomplete, or you missed a place, put the partially peeled paper back down and press the area again.

Photo Finishing

Tip

Alternatively, consider expanding the margins, and including a white "mat" around each photo transfer.

1

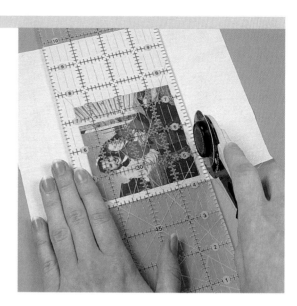

Using a rotary cutter, ruler, and mat, trim each side of the completed photo transfer, leaving a *scant* ¼-inch seam allowance all around. That way, when you stitch the photo-transfer fabric into a quilt, the seam line will be slightly *inside* the image area and will keep white lines from showing after the seams are pressed. Make sure to trim the photo-transfer fabric so it's square. That way, your patchwork will go together easily. The photo-transfer fabric will not stretch and be as forgiving as regular quilting cottons.

2

Stitch a photo-transfer block as you would any other quilt block, with two exceptions: Insert pins only in the seam allowance areas of the photo image, since pins can leave permanent holes in the image area. Also, sewing machines move the bottom layer of fabric under the presser foot faster than they move the top layer of fabric, so **place the photo transfer (which will not stretch) on top, and regular quilting cotton fabric, cut as precisely as possible, on the bottom.** This will ease in any fullness automatically.

3

If you've used Photos-To-Fabric transfer paper, you may press your stitched blocks on the right side. Note that not all transfer papers will produce a photo transfer that can be ironed this way. Be sure to refer to the manufacturer's packaging for pressing instructions, and be aware that some transfers cannot be pressed at all. Also follow the care and cleaning instructions so your finished images maintain clarity over time.

The Quilter's
Problem Solver

Photos in a Fog

Problem	Solution
Your photo didn't transfer completely. There are white areas on the fabric where the picture should be.	If your iron is working properly and is on the right setting, the culprit might be your ironing surface. Instead of using your ironing board, wrap two layers of quilt batting around a piece of shelving or a flat board. Then cover the batting with a piece of cotton fabric. This will provide just enough (but not too much) padding. Put it on the floor to get the best leverage. And remember—the harder you push, the better your transfer will be.
You accidentally made a pinhole in a photo-transfer patch.	Press it with the tip of your iron to make it less noticeable.

Skill Builder

Think big! Make photo-transfers that are up to 8 × 10½ inches in size (or the full size of the transfer paper).

If the image you want to transfer is larger than the sole plate of your iron, press it in sections. Press each section for 30 seconds, sliding the iron to keep the steam vents from resting in the same place for too long. Then move to the next section. Remember which parts of the transfer you've pressed and which parts you have not pressed, since the appearance of the back of the transfer paper won't tell you. One way to remember is to trace the outline of the iron onto the transfer paper with a pencil before moving it to the next section.

Try This!

For something different, turn a normal photograph into a silhouette.

You can do this before making the color copy onto transfer paper, if you don't mind cutting your photograph. You can also do it after your trip to the photocopy machine, just prior to ironing the transfer. It's a great way to get rid of dark and uninteresting backgrounds, or to remove parts of a photographic image. Just remember that the background will then be the same color as the fabric onto which you transfer your photo.

MAKING MEMORIES

A

Acrylic ruler. A thick, clear measuring tool, indispensable for rotary cutting. They come in a wide variety of sizes. A square ruler is handy for squaring up blocks and cutting perfectly square corners.

Appliqué. Attaching small pieces of fabric to a larger background fabric by hand or machine stitching.

B

Background overlay. A piece of background fabric used in reverse applique. The shape is cut out of the background, which is then stitched over a fabric-covered foundation.

Backstitch. Taking a second stitch back over a stitch that has already been taken, to secure a hand-pieced seam at the beginning or end.

Batting. The "invisible" layer in the center of a quilt. Usually made of cotton, polyester, or wool, batting is available in a variety of thicknesses. The fiber content of the batting dictates how close or far apart the quilt can be quilted to retain its shape, as well as how the finished quilt needs to be laundered.

Bias. The stretchy, diagonal line of the fabric. True bias is at a 45-degree angle to the straight grain, but any off-grain cut may be referred to as a bias cut.

C

Corner Cutters. The corner triangle portions of a framed block that are trimmed off and replaced with a pieced unit. Corner cutters unify a quilt design, while the framing strips make slightly inconsistent block sizes uniform.

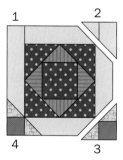

1   2
4   3

Couching. Machine or hand stitching a decorative yarn, thread, or other bulky trim onto the surface of fabric. It is used when the thread is too bulky to feed through the sewing machine.

Crazy quilting or crazy piecing. The process of constructing a randomly pieced block from irregularly shaped scraps of fabric. A foundation material such as paper or muslin is usually used to give the block stability.

Crosswise grain. The grain formed by the weft threads that run perpendicular to the selvages. The fabric along grain is fairly stable and has a minimal amount of stretch.

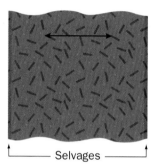
Selvages

Cutwork lace. Reverse appliquéing a top layer of fabric with many cutout areas to an underneath layer of fabric, to create the look of openwork lace.

D

Darning foot. A presser foot with a large opening at its base. The base may be circular or horseshoe-shaped, clear plastic or metal. Used during free-motion stitching or free motion quilting, this foot moves up and down with the needle, holding fabric in place when the needle is down, but allowing free motion of the piece when the needle is in the up position.

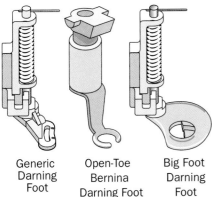

Generic Darning Foot   Open-Toe Bernina Darning Foot   Big Foot Darning Foot

Decorative stitching. Visible stitching added to fabric for detail and texture, rather than for joining pieces. Stitching may be done by hand or machine using silk, rayon, metallic, or other unusual threads, yarns, and ribbons.

Dimensional appliqué. Appliqué in which the pieces rise above the surface of the background fabric. Fabric may be folded, gathered, or stuffed to achieve a three-dimensional look. Dimensional appliqué is especially popular in album-style quilts.

Focus fabric. A multicolor fabric (often a floral print), that can help suggest color schemes for quilts.

Foundation. Either a permanent (muslin, woven interfacing) or temporary (paper, nonwoven interfacing) material that provides a base for crazy piecing. A foundation may also be used to stabilize a

quilt that will be heavily embellished.

Framing strip. Strips of fabric that are added to blocks, making individual borders all around.

Free-motion stitching. Machine stitching done with the feed dogs down, a lessening of the thread tension, and a darning foot on the machine, allowing you to stitch in any direction you choose.

Freezer paper. A roll of household paper with one plastic-coated side. Its original purpose was for freezing foods, but quilters have carried it off to the sewing room for foundation piecing, template making, and appliqué.

Fusible web. An adhesive product, usually with a peel-off paper backing that allows you to bond appliqués to a background or any two pieces of fabric together. Heat from a dry iron melts the adhesive to secure the bond.

Heliotropic. Characterized as being effected by the influence of sunlight. Because they are heliotropic, plants tend to grow toward the light; heliotropic paints produce more vivid colors where the sun has shone directly on them.

Lengthwise grain. The warp threads, or straight of grain parallel to the

selvages. This grain direction is the most stable. It is virtually unstretchable.

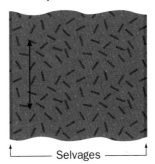

— Selvages —

Loft. The amount of puffiness in a batting. Batting can vary from very low loft to high or extra loft.

Log Cabin block. A block constructed by adding strips around a center shape, traditionally a square.

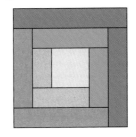

Milliner's needle. A long, thin needle used for appliqué. This needle can also be used to join pieces of batting. It is longer and more flexible than other needles.

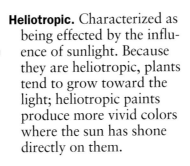

Patchwork. Small pieces of fabric sewn together to form a larger unit, quilt block, or quilt top.

Photo transfer. The process of copying a photographic image onto fabric.

G L O S S A R Y

Q

Quilt sandwich. The three layers of a quilt, including the quilt top, the middle layer of batting, and the backing.

R

Reverse appliqué. An appliqué technique where attention is paid to finishing the cut-out, negative spaces of an appliqué shape, to let the background show through.

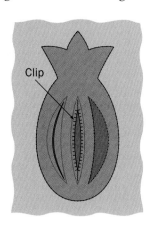

Clip

Rotary cutter. A fabric-cutting tool that resembles a pizza cutter, but with a razor-sharp blade. Used in conjunction with an acrylic ruler, it makes straight cuts and is capable of slicing through several layers of fabric at once.

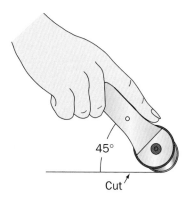

45°

Cut

Ruching. From the French, a term that means gathering, ruffling, or pleating. Ruched embellishments can be found on both quilts and garments from earlier times and have enjoyed a great revival in the late twentieth century.

Running stitches. Short stitches taken by inserting a needle into and out of two layers of fabric at regular intervals. Used for hand piecing or basting.

S

Sandpaper board. A rectangular sheet of sturdy material such as plastic or masonite that has a piece of fine-grit sandpaper glued to one side. The hard, nonslip surface is helpful for keeping fabric steady when marking around hand piecing or appliqué templates.

Silk pins. Long, very thin straight pins that glide through fabrics easily. These straight pins leave virtually no holes in the fabric when they are removed.

Stem stitch. Embroidery stitch used to outline a shape. Stem stitch is a variation of outline stitch and is usually rendered with two or three strands of embroidery floss.

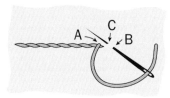

Stem stitch

Stipple quilting. Very closely spaced, random lines of free-motion machine quilting that create a pattern resembling a jigsaw puzzle. In larger scale, called Meander quilting.

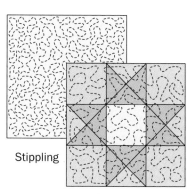

Stippling

Meandering

Straight grain. The lengthwise or crosswise threads in the weave of fabric.

Straw needles. Long, thin needles with narrow shanks, used for hand appliqué.

Strings. Long, rotary-cut strips of fabric for piecing. Strings are often cut so they taper from narrow at one end to wider at the opposite end.

T

Template. An exact copy of a pattern piece, usually constructed from a sturdy material like template plastic so that it can be traced around many times without distorting its shape. Commonly used in appliqué and piecing, templates are also used in quilting, where a simple motif is cut from plastic, then traced around onto the quilt top.

Trapunto. A method where stitched designs are stuffed with extra batting to provide dimension and a sculptural effect.

U_____

Utility knife. Also referred to as a craft knife, or by the brand name X-Acto; available at art supply and hardware stores. The smallest blade, #1, is handy for making small slits in fabric and cutting through template plastic.

Z_____

Zigzag stitch. The machine stitch used for satin stitching and sometimes machine appliqué. The needle swings from the left to the right as the stitch advances. The width of the stitch can be modified from very narrow to very wide.

Zipper foot. A specialty sewing machine presser foot. In applying piping, its design enables you to stitch very close to the cord.

**Tulip Pattern
(Actual Size)
for
"Revival Techniques"
on page 82**

Diane Bartels is a fiber artist and quiltmaker with a 26-year history of working with color and textiles. After learning how to do a Log Cabin quilt, she started dyeing her own cottons because commercial fabrics did not meet her needs. The techniques Diane uses in creating textile art range from low tech (making screens, stamps, and stencils by hand) to high tech (using a digital scanner, computer, and printer).

Cynthia A. Blackberg won the International Quilt Festival's Jewel Pearce Patterson Award for teaching excellence in 1993. In 1995, she was nominated for *The Professional Quilter* magazine's Teacher of the Year award. In addition, she is a co-founder of The Florida Handwork Gathering, a unique seminar held in Mt. Dora, Florida, that is dedicated to developing fine handwork skills.

Georgia J. Bonesteel is the creator and host of the television program *Lap Quilting*. Georgia shares her expertise through the Spinning Spools pattern club and through teaching during weeklong retreats at Freedom Escape Lodge in Weaverville, North Carolina, and the Nine Quarter Circle Ranch in Gallatin Gateway, Montana. She is the author of seven books, most recently *Lap Quilting Lives*. Georgia operates The Quilt Corner in downtown Hendersonville, North Carolina.

Karen Kay Buckley is the author of four books published with the American Quilter's Society. She is a member of the National Quilting Association, the American Quilter's Society, and the International Quilt Association. She is very active with her local guild, the Letort Quilters, and was selected as Teacher of the Year by *The Professional Quilter* magazine in 1997.

Elsie M. Campbell began exhibiting her quilts in 1992 and has been teaching quiltmaking since 1994. She holds a Bachelor of Science in home economics education and a Masters in special education. She was a public school teacher until February 1999, when she accepted a position as editor at Chitra Publications, publisher of *Miniature Quilts, Quilting Today*, and *Traditional Quiltworks* magazines.

Karen Combs is an author, teacher, and quilt designer who is well known for her quilts of illusion. She is in demand as a teacher who encourages her students and makes learning fun. She is the author of *Optical Illusions for* Quilters, *3-D Fun with Pandora's Box*, and *Combing through Your Scraps*. In addition, she has appeared on the TV programs *Quilting from the Heartland* and *Simply Quilts*, and she has written numerous articles about her quilting techniques.

Sharyn Craig was named the first Quilt Teacher of the Year in 1985 by *The Professional Quilter* magazine. She is the author of nine books and many magazine articles on quiltmaking. The title of her most recent book, co-authored with Harriet Hargrave, is *The Art of Classic Quiltmaking*. She is the creator of the "Design Challenge" column for *Traditional Quiltworks* magazine, in which she challenges readers to be innovative in exploring design opportunities.

Jill Sutton Filo is a self-taught graphic artist. In 1993, she began research on Ruby Short McKim, who was instrumental in reviving quilting in the 1920s. Jill's findings were presented at the American Quilt Study Group's national conference, and published in *Uncoverings 1996*. Jill currently publishes pattern books, lectures, and continues her research. *Better Homes and Gardens American Patchwork and Quilting* magazine published a series of her articles and patterns.

Laura Heine won the 1994 Bernina Award for best machine workmanship at the American Quilter's Society Competition in Paducah, Kentucky. She teaches for YLI, and her quilts are featured in their ads and brochures. Laura also designs fabrics for Kings Road Imports; her recent line of fabric is called "Fondly Flowers." Laura has combined efforts with stained glass artist Dione Roberts to make quilts from stained glass patterns, such as "Spool of Thread" on pages 4 and 96.

Jeana Kimball is a prolific author of quiltmaking books, including *Reflections of Baltimore, Red and Green, Appliqué Borders, Loving Stitches, Fairmeadow, Rabbit Patch, Come Berrying*, and *Backyard Garden*. She has also designed fabric for Marcus Brothers Textiles and has done commissioned work. Jeana travels nationally and internationally, sharing her love of quilting through classes and lectures.

Suzanne Marshall is the winner of the Gingher Award at the American Quilter's Society in Paducah, Kentucky. She is the author of *Take-Away Appliqué,* and she teaches and lectures throughout the United States, and in South Africa and Australia. Her quilt "Toujours Nouveau" was selected as one of the Twentieth Century's 100 Best American Quilts.

Linda Pool has taught classes and lectured on quilting techniques in many interest areas. She was a winner in three of the Great American Quilt Contests sponsored by The Museum of American Folk Art in New York City. She was the Virginia state winner in the Memories of Childhood crib quilt contest, garnering a special award for the most imaginative use of detail. Her quilts, patterns, and articles have been published in numerous quilting books and magazines. She was a member of the staff of the Jinny Beyer Hilton Head Island Quilting Seminar for 10 years. Linda also teaches and serves as a judge at quilt and needlework shows.

Sally Schneider is a designer and teacher, and she has been a quilt book editor at That Patchwork Place and Rodale Inc. She is the author of *Scrap Happy, Painless Borders,* and *Traditional Quilts with Painless Borders.* As a designer, one of her favorite methods is to start with a traditional pattern and play with different arrangements, sometimes rotating the design to face the opposite direction. Her creativity and innovative approaches to machine piecing and scrap quilts have made her classes instant hits with students throughout the country.

Anita Shackelford is an internationally known teacher and lecturer. She has won eleven Best of Show awards and many awards for workmanship. Two of her quilts have received the Mary Krickbaum Award for best hand quilting at a National Quilting Association show. Anita is the author of *Three-Dimensional Appliqué and Embroidery Embellishment: Techniques For Today's Album Quilt, Anita Shackelford: Surface Textures,* and *Appliqué with Folded Cutwork,* all published by the American Quilter's Society. Under the business name of Thimble Works, she designs patterns and tools, such as the RucheMark Circular Ruching Guides.

Ami Simms is the author of eight books on quilting, including three on photo transfer, and more than 50 articles for national quilting publications. She is the creator of the "Worst Quilt in the World Contest." Ami has made almost 100 quilts of varying sizes, in both traditional and contemporary designs. On national television, Ami has been a featured guest on the *Home & Family Show* and Alex Anderson's *Simply Quilts.* She hosts an internet chat for quilters and writes an online newsletter every month.

Susan Stein has owned two quilt shops, chaired a national quilt show, been elected state guild president, and taught both locally and nationally. Susan has designed projects for the four Singer Sewing Library quilting books and many other publications. She is the author of a book of her own patterns and is currently working on a book on Double Wedding Ring designs.

Mary Stori is the author of *The Wholecloth Garment Stori* and *The Stori Book of Embellishing,* and has been featured in 19 quilt magazines and other publications. Mary has appeared on HGTV's *Simply Quilts* and *Sew Perfect* several times. She designed the Mary Stori Collection for Kona Bay Fabrics and her own line of trapunto quilting stencils for Quilting Creations. She travels worldwide to present lectures, workshops, fashion shows of her wearables, and to host tours for quilters.

Eileen Jahnke Trestain designs her own patterns and markets them under the name Peonies Needlework. Her work has been published in *Patchwork and Quilting* in Great Britain. She is the author of *Dating Fabrics—A Color Guide: 1800-1960.* Eileen is the founding president of the Phoenix Area Quilter's Association. She is an appraiser of quilted textiles, certified by the AQS in 1991. She appraises, judges, and teaches about vintage quilts and fabrics, home care of quilts, and other subjects related to quilting.

Beth Wheeler is a freelance designer in sewing and craft areas. Beth's art garments and quilts have been in numerous invitational shows, museum exhibits, and are in private collections across the country. Her company, Beth Wheeler Creative Services, has recently expanded to include a line of craft and quilting patterns and kits. Beth is the author of more than 20 how-to project books.

Darra Duffy Williamson is the author of *Sensational Scrap Quilts* and has written many magazine articles. In 1989, Darra was named Quilt Teacher of the Year by *The Professional Quilter* magazine. Her colorful, multifabric quilts are award winners on local, regional, and national levels. She freelances as a technical writer, editor, and research consultant. Darra's column, "Traditional with a Twist," ran for 3 years in *Quilting Today* magazine.

Acknowledgments

Quilt Artists

We gratefully thank the following quiltmakers who graciously permitted us to show their original designs in this book:

Diane Bartels, Footprints of Summer II, 1997, on page 86.

Cynthia A. Blackberg, Sunflower Quilt, 1998, on page 42.

Georgia J. Bonesteel, Americana wall hanging, Stars and Strips jacket, on page 8.

Karen Kay Buckley, Opulent Ornaments, 1999, on page 24.

Elsie M. Campbell, Aunt Mimi's Triumph (Whig's Defeat), 1999, on page 90.

Karen Combs, Stairway to the Stars, 1997, on page 30.

Sharyn Craig, Better Cheddar, 1999, on page 36.

Jill Sutton Filo, Ruby's Flower Garden Tulip pillow, 1999, on page 82.

Laura Heine, Spool of Thread, 1999, on page 96.

Jeana Kimball, Hexagon Rose, 2000, on page 54.

Suzanne Marshall, Earth Watch, 1997, on page 60.

Sally Schneider, Kaleidoscope, 1999, on page 12.

Anita Shackelford, Flowers from Friends, 1998, on page 72.

Ami Simms, Family Fotos, 1998, on page 114.

Susan Stein, Fruit Basket Upset, 1999, on page 76.

Mary Stori, But, Dr.!!, 1993, on page 102.

Beth Wheeler, vest, 2000, on page 48.

Darra Duffy Williamson, Still Life #1, 1999, cover detail and page 18.

Sample Makers and Providers

Thanks to all of the above quiltmakers and Linda Dease Smith for providing samples. In addition to Anita Shackelford, the following quilters worked on Flowers from Friends: Glenda Clark, Janet Hamilton, Sheila Kennedy, Ruth Kennedy, Jo Lischynski, Connie St. Clair, and Rebecca Whetstone. The quilt is shown here courtesy of Sheila Kennedy.

Two redwork pillow shams on page 82, c. 1900-1910, are courtesy of Jill Sutton Filo.

The scrap quilt on pages 108-112, c. 1940, is courtesy of Eileen Jahnke Trestain.

Thanks to the Zephyr Gallery in Peddler's Village, Lahaska, Pennsylvania, for lending us the kaleidoscope by Mike Mason, on page 12.

Supplies

American & Efird, Inc.—Mettler threads, Signature machine quilting threads

Bernina of America, Inc.—Virtuosa 150 sewing machine

Big Board—large ironing board

Clotilde, Inc.—quiltmaking supplies

Dharma Trading Company—Setacolor Transparent paints

Omnigrid, Inc.—acrylic rulers and cutting mats

Rowenta—professional iron

Resources

Georgia Bonesteel
P.O. Box 96
Flat Rock, NC 28731
www.georgiabonesteel.com
Grid Grip

Karen Combs' Studio
1405 Creekview Court
Columbia, TN 38401
www.karencombs.com
60-degree diamond templates, isometric graph paper

Dharma Trading Company
P.O. Box 150916
San Raphael, CA 94915
(415) 456-7657
catalog@dharmatrading.com
www.dharmatrading.com
Setacolor Transparent paints by Pebeo, natural and bleached white fabrics in yardage, ready-made products

Laura Heine
Fiberworks
1310 24th St. West
Billings, MT 59102
(406) 656-6663
www.fiberworks-heine.com
Spool of Thread pattern

Jeana Kimball
Foxglove Cottage
P.O. Box 18294
Salt Lake City, UT 84118
Straw needles, appliqué patterns

The Kirk Collection
1513 Military Avenue
Omaha, NE 68111
(800) 398-2542
www.kirkcollection.com
Fabric and threads for repairing quilts, crepeline, vintage fabrics

Linda Pool
P.O. Box 523
Oakton, VA 22124
lpoolquilts@aol.com
"Very Victorian" cutwork lace appliqué patterns

Anita Shackelford
1539 Fairview Ave.
Bucyrus, OH 44820
anita@thimbleworks.com
RucheMark guides for dimensional appliqué

Ami Simms
Mallery Press, LLC
4206 Sheraton Dr.
Flint, MI 48532
(800) 278-4824
mallerypress@aol.com
www.mallerypress.com
Photos-to-Fabric transfer paper, 200 thread-count fabrics, photo transfer kits

Index

INDEX

Quilting Styles

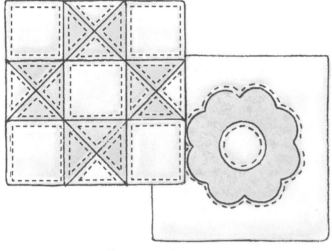

Outline Quilting

Echo Quilting

Single

Double

Crosshatch or Grid Quilting

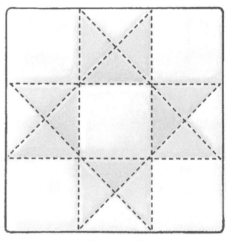

In the Ditch Quilting

Stipple Quilting

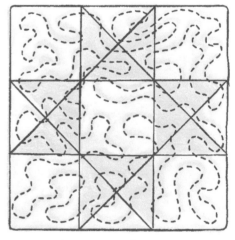

Meander Quilting